European Foundation for the Improvement of Living and Working Conditions

Family Care of the Older Elderly: Casebook of Initiatives

EF/93/29/EN

European Foundation for the Improvement of Living and Working Conditions

Family Care of the Older Elderly: Casebook of Initiatives

by
M.A.G.A. Steenvoorden
F.G.E.M. van der Pas
N.G.J. de Boer
NIZW (Netherlands Institute of Care and Welfare)

Loughlinstown House,
Shankill, Co. Dublin, Ireland
Tel: +353 1 282 6888   Fax: +353 1 282 6456

Cataloguing data can be found at the end of this publication

Luxembourg: Office for Official Publications of the European Communities, 1993

ISBN 92-826-6572-0

© European Foundation for the Improvement of Living and Working Conditions, 1993

For rights of translation or reproduction, applications should be made to the Director, European Foundation for the Improvement of Living and Working Conditions, Loughlinstown House, Shankill, Co. Dublin, Ireland.

Printed in Ireland

FOREWORD

All over Europe partners, daughters, daughters-in-law, sons, parents-in-law, friends and acquaintances, in this order, care for the elderly. Partly thanks to them the elderly can stay in their own homes, have company and keep in touch with the outside world. Mostly untrained, they help with the daily physical care, eating, drinking and sleeping. For many of them this is a great physical and emotional burden, which is a heavy weight on their shoulders every day. It governs their private life. Some carers resign from their jobs in order to care for someone.

In many cases there are few problems, but the physical and emotional burden may become so great that the carer runs into problems himself. It is evident that among carers there is not only a great need for recognition of their efforts, but also for practical, emotional and social support.

In all European Community member states steps are taken to support the carer. This book includes fourteen examples of projects from EC member states. They show a great diversity of support and practical situations. It is intended that these practical examples are a source of inspiration for projects that support and relieve carers of the elderly.

PREFACE

The implications of an ageing population for both living and working conditions have occupied an important place in the European Foundation's programmes of work over the last decade. In particular, an extensive analysis of the situation of older people in the European Community was published in 1987 as **Meeting the Needs of the Elderly**. This report showed that the population of people over pension age and especially those aged 80 and over, is rising in all EC countries; it drew attention to the needs for care and support for these older elderly. The current studies have specifically looked at the situation of those who provide most of the care to dependent older people - their families, especially spouses and daughters.

The Foundation's studies have sought to document systematically the needs and experiences of these family carers, and to assess the impact of caring on daily life. Research was undertaken in all Member States, with the exception of Luxembourg. These national studies look, in particular, at policy developments and initiatives to assist family carers, with a view to identifying what can be done to improve the quality of life for carers, as well as for their dependent older relatives. Of course the nature and extent of supportive services varies significantly between the Member States, even though they share a common emphasis upon maintaining older people at home, in the community, for as long as possible.

This casebook of initiatives to support family carers represents an effort to sharpen the focus upon what can be, and is being, done to help family carers. It includes documentation of policies and practices in the Member States, covering initiatives in home services, respite care, support groups, day care, information and training. These initiatives were selected as positive illustrations and are presented using a common format that is designed to offer practical rather than comprehensive detail. The initiatives demonstrate the contribution of voluntary, private and public sectors and partnerships between them; a contact address for further information has been added to each case description.

An evaluation committee of the Foundation's Administrative Board, composed of representatives of employers' organisation, trades unions and governments in the Member States, reviewed the report in September 1992, welcomed its practical orientation and encouraged its publication. It is one of several reports* on family care that the Foundation is pleased to contribute during this European Year of Older People and Solidarity between Generations.

Clive Purkiss
Director

* 1. Family care of dependent older people in the European Community
     Hannelore Jani-Le Bris

  2. Carers talking : Interviews with family carers of older dependent people in the European Community
     Elizabeth Mestheneos, Judith Triantafillou (eds.)

  3. Eldercare and employment : Workplace policies and initiatives to support workers who are carers
     Marina Hoffmann, George Leeson

TABLE OF CONTENTS   Page

Author's Preface

I. INTRODUCTION   1

II. FOURTEEN CASES   3

   1. THE WORKING GROUP OF FAMILY CARERS   3
      Never again silent workers
      National, Belgium

   2. A SITTING-IN SERVICE FOR CARERS   9
      A church organisation gives them a breather
      Copenhagen, Denmark

   3. LEAVE OF ABSENCE AND ALLOWANCES FOR CARERS   14
      Support for the carers of the seriously and
      terminally ill
      Province of Ribe, Denmark

   4. SUPPORT GROUPS FOR CARERS   19
      The art is to be neither too involved nor too distant
      Local, France

   5. BERLIN SERVICE CENTRE PERFORMS PIONEER WORK FOR CARERS   24
      The advantages of combining emotional support with
      practical support
      Berlin, Germany

   6. ADVICE BUREAU FOR CARERS   29
      Keeping emotional support separate from practical help
      Norderstedt, Germany

   7. HELP AT HOME   35
      Argyroupolis, Greece

   8. COMUNITÀ S. EGIDIO   40
      Professionals in voluntary work
      Rome, Italy

   9. HELPING DEMENTIA PATIENTS AND THEIR CARERS   45
      A study course: Beginning with the professionals in
      the interest of the carers
      Nijmegen, The Netherlands

  10. TEMPORARY HELP VIA A CALL-IN CENTRE
      Voluntary workers are not an extension of
      professional care
      Schiedam, The Netherlands   50

11. DAY CENTRES GO LOCAL   56
    Under increasing pressure from carers
    Lisbon, Portugal

12. THE PINES   61
    A home providing respite care in a small town
    Appleby-in-Westmorland, U.K.

13. THE CARERS NATIONAL ASSOCIATION   66
    A national organisation for carers
    National, U.K.

14. CHARTER OF THE RIGHTS OF CARERS   71
    International, Ireland

AUTHOR'S PREFACE

This casebook is one of the subprojects of the umbrella project "FAMILY CARE FOR THE OLDER ELDERLY" that is set up by the European Foundation for the Improvement of Living and Working Conditions. This publication is a collection of fourteen descriptions of initiatives and projects concerned with the support of carers throughout the European Community (EC). This book is meant to be a practical rather than an exhaustive illustration of the various ways in which member states have interpreted the provision of support to carers. It may also serve as a source of inspiration for setting up new projects. It is therefore eminently suitable for organisations and government bodies which wish to initiate activities for the support of family care and are, in this context, seeking practical examples. Moreover, this casebook is a plea directed at politicians to work seriously on a national and European policy to support the position of the carers.

Working Method
In 1990 the European Foundation for the Improvement of Living and Working Conditions commissioned the `Nederlands Instituut voor Zorg en Welzijn' / NIZW (The Netherlands Institute for Care and Welfare) to compile this publication.
The realisation that a European policy was needed to cope with the situation of carers in Europe was the basis upon which the European Foundation for the Improvement of Living and Working Conditions set up the project "FAMILY CARE FOR THE OLDER ELDERLY" (Work Programme No. 26/1990(89)-5.2). One aim of this project was to investigate the situation of the carers of the elderly over 75 and a second was to gather ideas for the eventual improvement of their lot. Not only by formulating recommendations but also by describing projects and initiatives which are directed towards, or are very helpful in, the support of carers.
The research was carried out in eleven EC member states and the results were published in national reports. The general reports are based on a study of documentation on the situation of the elderly over 75 and their carers, interviews with carers and two or three case studies of initiatives per member state.

This research is incorporated in two publications. CLEIRPPA in Paris produced a description of the situation of the carers in the various EC member states under the title "Family Care of the Older Elderly in the European Community". The case studies are incorporated by the NIZW in this publication entitled "Family Care of the Older Elderly: Casebook of Initiatives".

The Danish institute 'Danage Foundation' takes care of a third publication. This study contains an inventory of the policies and initiatives of companies in EC member countries to support their employees in their role as carers.

In the context of this casebook, the researchers in the member states were asked to describe a number of initiatives in their countries. Each initiative or project was required to meet four criteria (EUF Protocol, December 1990):

i. it was specially created, or very useful, for the support of carers;
ii. it must have proved its right to existence;
iii. it must not require any large extra amounts of time, money or manpower;
iv. as far as possible, it should make use of both professional and voluntary workers

For purposes of clarity and comparison, they were asked to describe the initiatives, using 13 points of reference:

- target group;
- what is provided;
- the organisation;
- the workers;
- size and area served;
- accessibility;
- publicity;
- collaboration including contacts;
- funding;

- cost to client;
- experiences and problems;
- significance to the carer;
- recommendations for use elsewhere in Europe.

A selection of the descriptions thus obtained was finally included in this casebook.

The following principles were applied in making this selection:
- preferably at least one project per participating country;
- as many different kinds of projects as possible, both as regards organisation and the kind of support given;
- the project should be of interest to as many other EC countries as possible.

Account was taken of the projects which would be of special interest to southern European countries and those which would be of more interest to the northern countries. In this way, the description of the day care project in Lisbon would be more relevant to countries such as Spain and (Southern) Italy but less so to a country like Denmark where daycare is already part of the services provided.

Lastly, pragmatic considerations also played a role in the selection: if the report on any project was not sufficiently detailed, it could not be accepted for inclusion in the final selection.

Unfortunately it was impossible to adapt and incorporate the project descriptions from Spain in this casebook in time, because of communication problems.

The initiatives in this casebook are classified in alphabetic order and not according to the kind of support given, i.e. practical, emotional or material (by emotional support is meant special attention and appreciation so that the carer feels someone understands and values the work). The provision of information on the patient's illness or disability is also included. Practical support is concerned with 'instrumental' help, i.e.

with the household tasks or with the patient's personal needs. Finally, material support includes financial compensation and the provision of aids and equipment.

The majority of the initiatives are a combination of all three types of support. In Denmark, for instance, the sitting-in service provides not only practical support but is also an emotional support for the carer; the voluntary worker who comes to take over also lends a listening ear to what the carer has to say.

The final text was compiled by Mr. N.G.J. de Boer (journalist), Mrs. M.A.G.A. Steenvoorden (NIZW) and Mr. F.G.E.M. van der Pas (NIZW). The descriptions of the cases included were edited by Mr. N.G.J. de Boer. In doing so, he tried, as much as possible, to write the descriptions in the same style and to give them the same length. He removed ambiguities from these and where necessary further enquiries were made from the original authors.

We thank all researchers for handing in their case descriptions. Their efforts, involvement and ideas have been responsible for making this casebook one of both inspirational and practical value.

I. INTRODUCTION

In Europe, an increasing number of the elderly remain in the next few years in their own homes even if they need some kind of assistance to do so. To keep their independency they have to rely on care and attention of the institutionalized services, but also on the support of family, friends and volunteers and that is what this book is about. There are three basic reasons for this development. Firstly, the number of the elderly in Europe is likely to increase considerably in the coming decades. Apart from that, policies in nearly all EC member states want the elderly to live independently as long as possible and to be as independent as possible on care service by professionals, whereas family, friends, neighbours (carers) and volunteers will have to contribute more to the care of the elderly. Moreover, many elderly people would like to function as long as possible in their own environment and elderly people who need care can only do so with help from relatives, neighbours, friends, i.e. carers.

Whereas the demand for more care increases, its availability decreases and care is no longer taken for granted. This is influenced by various social developments: the decreasing number of children, more one-person households, the increase of geographic mobility and more women working. Attitudes to caring are also under discussion. For example, the women's movement has expressed criticism of the notion that more care should be provided by family members, neighbours and friends, since this usually falls upon women's shoulders.

These changes necessitate the development of policies and measures aimed at the judicious use of the care that is available. This need is felt to some extent in all the EC member states; a policy on caring is required not only at the national level but also at European level.

There is still not enough recognition of the specific significance of the efforts of carers to enable the elderly to live as long and as independently as possible in their own homes. If carers are to maintain their efforts, more projects that support them and relieve them of their practical work have to be initiated. Moreover, the personal relationship between carer and the person who is cared for is a very special one. This requires tailored emotional and social-psychological support. The third area of policy is the support of the social-economic position of carers. Because of their efforts as carers, they can not be (completely) economically independent, simply because they do not earn any money during the time they care for someone. Apart from that they experience difficulties in finding a paid job again after the care period. A fundamental problem is the protection of carer interests. Carers have to do this themselves, but in practice they hardly have time to do so. Therefore the position of the carer is a political issue and problem.

This casebook contains a diversity of projects throughout Europe. No matter in what form these projects are presented, it will not do justice to the individual character of each one. They all support the carers but the way they do it differs.

Some projects are remarkable since they offer chiefly practical assistance to the carers and to the elderly themselves. Examples of this are the sitting-in services in Denmark and the Netherlands, and the projects in Greece, Italy and Portugal which are attempting to provide a comprehensive service in people's homes. Other projects are interesting because they offer the carers actual psyco-social and emotional support, such as the support groups in France and the counselling bureau in Germany. These projects are different again from other projects which approach the problems of carers in an integrated fashion, such as the Berlin Service Centre and the British project, The Pines. These two differ again from each other; Berlin is a large city and The Pines is situated in a village. The Netherlands project in Nijmegen consciously trains professionals who have dealings with the carers in client situations. The Danish arrangement for carers' leave of absence and allowances come into a completely different category, aiming as they do to improve both the carer's income and the situation of combining work with caring. In Belgium and the UK the carers are organising themselves to represent their own interests and in Ireland a Declaration of Carers' Rights has been drawn up.

II. FOURTEEN PROJECTS

1. Belgium

THE WORKING GROUP OF FAMILY CARERS
Never again silent workers

The Working Group of Family Carers (de Werkgroep Thuisverzorgers)[1] was started in Belgium in 1988 on the initiative of the carers themselves. The main aim was to give carers some say in the care provided at home, in addition to what the professionals and the policy-makers would decide.

Up to that time, carers as a group, were unknown in Belgium. There were already patients' associations and self-help groups, and during the 1980s some institutions and health insurers had drawn up plans to assist carers. Nevertheless, the latter were left with the feeling that decisions were being made over their heads. The first booklet they issued was therefore called "Silent workers no longer".

The first impetus came in 1988 with a television programme on a "mantelzorg" project by the King Baudouin Foundation. The programme was tellingly entitled: "24 Hours a Day - the voice from within the home" and unleashed a flood of reactions. Many carers were found to have the same sort of problems: emotional, relations with other family members, insufficient understanding and sometimes even disapproval. Not all of them had adverse experiences with professional carers but there was clearly a deep divide between the professional services and possible alternatives.

The Working Group is especially important because it supports the family carers in their efforts to achieve recognition. Family caring is after all a valuable form of care with its own approach; within this approach the family carer is an important partner.

---

[1] In Belgium the term 'mantelzorg' also refers to organised voluntary workers; for this reason the term 'thuiszorgers' (home carers) is preferred. (Translator's note: in both the Dutch and Belgian reports the term 'family carer', or more often 'carer', has been used for the sake of uniformity).

The interests represented

The Working Group targets all 'families'[2] where those with a disability are cared for at home. It is not restricted to the carers of the elderly. The Working Group itself is composed of people who themselves look after a family member at home. This was a conscious choice on the part of the initiators.

The Working Group offers two kinds of services. Firstly, it aims to represent the interests of family carers both vis-à-vis the authorities and the various family care institutions. In addition, it offers a number of practical services.

At first the emphasis was very much on representation. By means of booklets, at conferences, through the media and unrelenting lobbying, the Working Group succeeded in turning the spotlight on the problems of carers. For this, the members of the Working Group worked from the assumption that everyone has the right to be cared for at home, even if quite a lot of help is needed. In order to ensure that this right is established, the general public, the authorities and the institutions will need a change of attitude. According to the Working Group, the general public wrongly assumes there are actually no longer any families who are prepared to take it on themselves to care for one of their members. Statistics show that, on the contrary, eighty per cent of the chronically ill are cared for at home. The politicians still have to get used to involving the family carers in the formulation of their policies. And professional institutions still have to learn to see family carers as partners in their work.

Special attention

A number of subjects received special attention in their representations:
- When the Government decided in 1986 that there should be more coordination in the area of family care, the Working Group succeeded in securing a place at the round table discussions, both regional and

---

2   For 'families', also read 'households'.

local. The carers were also allowed a permanent number of representatives on the Council for Family Care (an advisory body to the Flemish Government).
- The Working Group expresses its doubts about the payment of a fixed sum for the home care of those who need intensive nursing care. Previously the amount of this payment was arranged on an individual basis. A fixed sum might have meant, for example, fewer visits to the home by professional helpers.
- The Working Group also put forward improvements in the financial regulations for carers: tax concessions, allowances and compensation for career breaks.

The voice of the Working Group has not only been heard by Government but also by the services responsible for home care. In this context it acts as a consumer organisation, which occasionally evokes a defensive reaction from these services. Carers sometimes feel that they are approached too much as professionals when they would prefer to be regarded as partners who have developed special skills in the course of their caring. They would like to have more say in putting together the package of home care the patient is to receive. The care provided should be adapted more flexibly to the needs of the family carer; the latter should be able to call upon this outside office hours as well.

Direct support
In addition to representing their interests, the Working Group also aims to offer direct support to carers. This might be of a social or emotional nature, and provided by regional or local support groups. The object is to bring people together on a regular basis to strengthen their feelings of solidarity. The Working Group tries to help by this means to get the carers to act more resiliently in their own situations (even if only to ask for help from others in good time). The Working Group also provides practical services:
- A telephone number permanently manned for information and advice;
- Expertise in the area of management;
- A quarterly Newsletter;
- Help with training courses offered by professional bodies.

Internal organisation

The initiative for the Working Group came from two carers - a married couple - after the 1988 television programme. The Self-Help Centre at the University of Louvain offered to function as a "P.O. Box" where the viewers' reactions were collected. Anyone who wrote in received a reply, following which twelve people were found willing to take further action. The Working Group was officially recognised in 1990 as a non-profit-making organisation.

With its name "Working Group" - instead, for example, of Association - the initiators wish to convey that they are making a cautious beginning. The use of the term 'family carers' also has a purpose. By its use, the Working Group wish to emphasise the role of the family which, after all, takes upon itself the lion's share of the caring while other categories of helper (relatives, friends, neighbours, voluntary workers) only offer their services now and again.

At first, the Working Group received support from the Self-Help Centre but since 1990 it has received a government grant for a part-time professional to do the administrative work, organise the local meetings, look up information on request and edit the quarterly newsletter. The members of the Working Group take collective responsibility.

The Working Group is mainly active in the Flemish region. The newsletter goes to some 2,500 subscribers, six hundred of whom are family carers, and also to a large number of facilities and workers in the health services. The number is growing. There are seven local groups active in Flanders.

In addition to Government subsidy, the Group covers its expenses by income from subscriptions and donations. The participants have no other expenses. The members of the Working Group would like to have a paid assistant in each of the five provinces of Flanders.

Accessibility

The Working Group may be reached by telephone five days a week; in addition there are about ten other contact persons spread throughout Flanders. If there is any problem in making contact it is usually from the other side: carers hesitate to get in touch. This may have something to do with the isolation in which families live. Many of them also regard care as a temporary problem, for which there is no solution anyway.

Through articles in the press, press conferences and advertising on local radio new carers and members come in on a daily basis. Local working groups also make new contacts by making house calls but it is difficult to obtain addresses.

Experiences
Judging by the reactions of families and the services, the growth of the number of subscribers to the newsletter and the invitations to come and give information, the Working Group is obviously fulfilling a need.

Relations with the home care organisations are not always the easiest: the Working Group places itself in the shoes of the consumer and this evokes defensive reactions. Nevertheless a better relationship is gradually growing.

Through the work of the Group, the carers are coming out of their isolation. Their problems are reaching the ears of authority more directly since the Working Group has a free hand in regard to the services and policy-makers. That the Working Group speaks on behalf of all family carers – and not only for those who make use of the services – means that attention is paid to new aspects, such as the need for some payment for to family carers who provide intensive care in the home. The Working Group is not only concerned to bring forward new views but also that the carers should be able to identify with an organisation which is their own. That they often lost hope and wore themselves out in the past, had after all a lot to do with their feelings of being quite alone with their burden.

Family carers, new style
People live longer and the consequences within the family are not always easy to deal with. Family carers are becoming more heavily burdened as a result. At the same time there is also a new generation of carers. They no

longer feel it is 'obvious' that those requiring assistance should remain in their own homes. Theirs is a more conscious choice to do the caring and accept the effects on their lifestyle (such as giving up their jobs). But that does mean that they wish to be recognised as an equal partner with the other providers of assistance. In this way the Working Group confronts the fact of caring with a new challenge: caring for people in need of help has, after all, become a requirement from society as a whole; no one can now take for granted that informal care is free of charge.

Although they may differ in many respects, carers have the same problems: too little free time, too little appreciation, and financial problems. So far, only two EC countries - the UK and Belgium - have organisations for family carers. The experiment in Belgium demonstrates that an organisation can be got off the ground in a relatively short time, which will point the way to the next step in the development of home caring.

More information :
VZW Werkgroep Thuisverzorgers
Groeneweg 151
B-3001 Heverlee
Tel: 016 227337

2. Denmark

A SITTING-IN SERVICE FOR CARERS
A Church organisation gives them a breather

The greater Copenhagen area has had a sitting-in service for carers for the past year and a half. The initiative came from a Church organisation, the 'Association of Parochial Helpers', but was heavily influenced by one person, Sister Ellen Dalgaard Jensen. The Sitting-in Service is a separate service from the leave of absence and allowances for carers - which movement is described elsewhere in this casebook - but fits into this admirably. In the rest of Denmark and in other Scandinavian countries the progress of the sitting-in service is being followed with great interest. Which is not surprising, since it is a project which could be set up elsewhere by fairly simple means.

Ellen Dalgaard Jensen worked abroad for many years, mainly in the United States. There she had close contacts with relatives of people who were seriously or terminally ill and realised that there was a group of people in great need of support. In 1989, back in Denmark, she developed her plan for a sitting-in service. She submitted it to the 'Association of Parochial Helpers' who at once showed interest and took up the suggestion. This association is composed of over a hundred people who perform various kinds of social work under the auspices of the Church, in the greater Copenhagen area. This work varies from house calls to lonely people to social counselling and moral support in crisis situations to courses for Church voluntary workers.

The Association also helps people coping with a bereavement and so they already knew how much support was needed by carers. This was also confirmed by the organisations with whom they subsequently had contact, the hospitals, social services, home care services and patients' associations. The need was great. Against this background, the sitting-in service came into being in 1990. Sister Ellen Dalgaard Jensen was employed to implement the plan. A group of voluntary workers was formed, information was disseminated and in September 1990 the service officially began.

Service provided

The sitting-in service is intended for the relatives of seriously or terminally ill patients. These are usually elderly people. Others may also avail of it but it is estimated that between half and three-quarters of the people are over seventy years of age. The object of the service is to allow the carer to get some relaxation and to pursue activities outside the home.

Anyone wishing to avail of the service applies to the Association of Parochial Helpers. The patient her/himself may do this, or the carer or anyone who feels that a sitter-in is needed in a given situation. Other family members, friends, district nurses, GPs or the clergy may get in touch with them, naturally only with the permission of the person concerned.

As soon as a call comes in, Sister Jensen pays a house call to arrange for the sitter to come. She finds out, among other things, whether others are already helping and exactly what kind of help is required.

The sitting-in service covers Copenhagen and surrounding area. During the past year the volunteers went to sit-in with approximately fifty families. At present they visit about twenty families. In total, they spend over a hundred hours a month sitting in. So far the service has succeeded in responding to all the incoming calls for help. The sitters spend a maximum of three hours a day in someone's home but if necessary will repeat this several times a week. During these hours they do no domestic work or nursing in the real sense of the word. What they do is remain close at hand and lend a listening ear to the elderly person. How long they continue to do so varies from situation to situation. In one case help will be required for a short period but on a fairly intensive basis - for example staying three hours several times a week with a dying person so that the carer can get some sleep. In other cases a sitter is needed at a fixed time each week to enable the carer to get out of the house for a bit.

The sitting-in service does not cost the elderly person or the carer anything, although the Association of Parochial Helpers will mention that help with travelling expenses is always welcome. The Association covers all the costs of the service, from Sister Jensen's salary to the printing of leaflets and the assistance of a secretary.

Internal organisation

Ellen Dalgaard Jensen works part-time (75%) for the sitting-in service. The work on the ground is carried on by almost forty unpaid volunteers. The original group of volunteers was mainly composed of ex-nurses and health workers. When they expanded they sought 'mature men and women with experience of life'. Before the voluntary workers are allowed to function they first have an interview with Ellen Dalgaard Jensen. Part of this is to discover what their motives are, whether they have experience of looking after the sick or dying, and how they might act in a crisis. Their own home situation and religious beliefs are also discussed. The volunteers are not required to be church members but are expected to support the aims of the organisation. Occasionally Sister Jensen has turned down a candidate because she did not feel he or she was sufficiently stable or well-balanced to do such demanding work. One of the candidates she refused, for example, was someone who was still trying to come to terms with a bereavement of her own.

Implementation

Each volunteer signs a promise to keep confidentiality. In addition the volunteers carry an identity card on all visits. There are regular training courses and support meetings. These deal with questions such as: How do you get a conversation going? How do you cope with the anguish, aggression and anger which is released when people are seriously ill? And how do you keep going in a crisis? How do you help AIDS sufferers? But also very practical questions are dealt with, like what regulations and entitlements exist in the area of social security.

As soon as a volunteer goes to work, Sister Jensen gets in touch with him or her to find out if all is going well or whether the volunteer concerned has come to the right place. This contact is kept up since the volunteer makes regular reports and from time to time Sister Jensen gets in touch by telephone.

The Association of Parochial Helpers organises a meeting once a month at which all the volunteers can exchange experiences. Several times a year a three-day course for beginners and experienced volunteers is held.

After a certain length of time Sister Jensen may consider it preferable to change to another volunteer. If the patient is dying this may be at the end of about a fortnight, if chronically ill, then after about a month. Sister Jensen feels it is right in any case to change the volunteer after about three months; a change of surroundings may act as an inspiration to the volunteer.

Information
As much information as possible about the sitting-in service is given out in order to keep relatives of the seriously ill and dying informed, but also to recruit new volunteers. This information is primarily provided through the official health services, the hospitals, welfare and district nursing services. But other organisations, such as Kræftens Bekæmpelse (an association for cancer patients) and Husligt Arbejdersforbund (a union of domestic workers), pass on information about the sitting-in service. Once the service had got going, person-to-person advertising was also effective. The newspapers and professional journals also gave it plenty of coverage and Sister Jensen has given numerous lectures on the subject. The experiences of the service are thus passed on to other people who are engaged in setting up a similar service elsewhere. Now that the Sitting-in Service has been in existence for a year and a half, the message has got through to all the relevant institutions and organisations in the health service and services for the elderly that they can make use of it.

Cooperation
Those working in the sitting-in service attach a great deal of value to cooperation with other organisations. Not only with the official health services and public facilities, but also with patients' associations like the Cancer and Multiple Sclerosis societies. These organisations often have in any case direct contact with carers. The Sitting-in Service also has close contacts with the home nursing services. Not because their volunteers take over some of their work, but just because they add something to it. After all, they have more time and, with their experience of life, have different things to offer.

Significance
The carers are very pleased with the sitting-in service. Some of them were almost on the point of collapse under the huge burden which a seriously or terminally ill relative can mean. One of them had not had a holiday in

sixteen years since she had always had to look after her ailing mother. Another confessed to Sister Jensen that she had had notions of suicide because she could no longer bear the physical and emotional pressure. The sitting-in service was a marvellous relief for them and for other carers. And yet such a praiseworthy initiative could quite easily be set up in other places, too. It is fairly inexpensive, since it employs mainly voluntary workers. If at a later stage there is a need for paid workers, each case can be considered individually as to where funding might be found.

The members of the Danish Sitting-in Service are emphatic that in setting up a similar project it is very important to keep in close contact with the local authority. The latter can then become involved and it also helps to establish what is the size of the target group.

==
More information :
Ms. Ellen Dalgaard Jensen
De Samvirkende Menighedsplejer
Valby Tingsted 7
DK-2500 Valby
Tel: 31 46 66 66
==

3. Denmark

LEAVE OF ABSENCE AND ALLOWANCES FOR CARERS
Support for the carers of the seriously and terminally ill

Dying in a hospital is less personal than coming to the end of life at home. Besides, it is often needlessly expensive. With this realisation, a plan was conceived in recent years in the Danish province of Ribe to offer support of various kinds to people who wished to undertake the care of seriously ill or dying relatives and friends. From 1 December 1989 the plan was put into operation on a trial basis for one year. Half-way through this pilot project the Danish Government rowed in with legislation to regulate this type of assistance by law. To the gratification of the carers, even though neither the provincial project nor the new legislation actually targets them directly.

It was the provincial authority of Ribe which took the initiative for the project in 1987. Together with the municipal authorities, the Council made plans to provide this service, which acts as an alternative to a hospital admission. General practitioners and hospitals reacted positively to it and it was started up at the end of 1989.

Target group and service provided
What was actually on offer? To begin with, this was financial compensation for those who cared for a sick person at home; by doing this they would lose at least part of their former income. But the municipal and provincial authorities were offering more:
- Round-the-clock home care or a nurse for relief duty, house calls or full-time duty; this provision was made even for municipalities where up to that time no 24-hour, 7- day nursing was available;
- Adaptation of homes;
- Respite care in a nursing home, for example to reduce nervous pressure on the carer;
- Free child care;
- Free medicines, aids and equipment;
- Regular collection of nursing waste;
- Special assistance, e.g. from consultants, psychologists, physiotherapists and psycho- therapists.

This service was originally intended for terminally ill patients who had less than a year to live and who could not do without constant care and attention. But indirectly it was also intended to benefit those who looked after the patient in his/her own home.

Normally, the district nurse was the person who assessed whether the terminal patient in question was prepared to avail of this service. Sometimes this decision was in the hands of the staff at a hospital where the patient had been admitted. And in three per cent of cases, the assessment was made by the carers themselves.

During the trial period, 361 people availed of one or more of these services. During the same period, 267 of these patients died. This is about 12% of all deaths during the same period. Age was not a selection criterion for being allowed to participate in the project. In practice, half the participants were aged over 70 years. Thirteen per cent of them were under 55, while 6% were over 84.

What it meant to the carers

Although the project was not specially intended for carers, it nevertheless meant a great deal to them. The leave of absence arrangement was particularly important. In 54 of the 361 cases the carers made use of this opportunity. Fourteen of these carers were men. Of these 54, 38 got full-time and 12 part-time leave of absence. In over half the cases the employer felt it was a good idea and cooperated willingly. The leave usually lasted less than three months; in only 7% of cases did it exceed four months.

In addition to the leave of absence, there was also the possibility of having the patient admitted to respite care. The carers found this especially attractive: 23 patients availed of this service, in more than half the cases in order to allow the carer to have some relief. In six cases it was necessary in the context of the terminal care to arrange for children to be looked after. In one case these were the carer's children, since she could not manage to look after her sick mother and her children at the same time.

In the background, in this project, was the idea that the decision to spend one's last days at home rather than in hospital ought not to entail any extra expense, either for the dying person or the carer. All the expenses which in the case of a hospital admission would be borne by the hospital were now borne by the municipal and provincial authorities. The same also applied to the income which the carer might lose by undertaking to care for an elderly person.

Experiences

The vast majority of those involved were satisfied with the project. The carers felt it was especially nice to be able to help the patient to have a dignified death in accordance with his or her own wishes. They found the terminal care a rather intensive period - often difficult and emotionally burdensome - but yet worthwhile. Some of them expressed their gratitude for the moral support they had received from the professionals (such as the home helps and district nurses). The fact that, day or night, they could also call for home care and that in emergencies it was always possible to have the patient admitted to hospital, was also a great standby.

The carers were less enthusiastic about the fact that after six in the evenings it was not possible to get any home help. Also, the information on the project was not always sufficient and problems sometimes occurred after a patient was discharged from hospital. There was also criticism of the lack of coordination between the various official services involved in terminal care. According to those delivering these, in ninety per cent of the cases there was no mention of any serious problem in this connection.

At national level, too

Halfway through the trial period, on 1 July 1990, the Danish legislature decided that it would now be possible to offer the same support to carers in other parts of the country as was being offered in Ribe. The new act also provides that anyone who is prepared to care for someone wishing to die in his/her own home can apply for compensation for loss of income thus incurred, i.e. a caring allowance. In order to receive this caring allowance, the hospital must issue a declaration that medical treatment offers the patient no further hope. The patient's condition should furthermore not be such as to necessitate his or her remaining in a hospital or other institution. Finally, the patient must also agree to be cared for in his/her own home.

The policy-makers assume that the caring allowance per case will need to be provided for between two and six months. The allowance is based on the average income of the carer during the previous twelve months, although a maximum has been fixed which corresponds to the maximum pay for domestic help plus an extra allowance which is fixed by each local authority. The carer retains the allowance even if the patient being cared for is admitted temporarily to hospital. The allowance can be discontinued, for example if the patient turns out to be no longer terminal. This seldom happens, however.

Rights

The legislation may create the opportunity for people to become carers, but this is not an automatic right; their employers must also be in agreement. Most collective agreements make provision for this. In addition, the Danish Government assumes that in any case employers in the public sector will have no objections. The Ministry in question has recommended, for example, that public servants and employees in subsidised schools and church institutions should be facilitated in taking leave for the purpose of caring.

Anyone who 'is so close to the patient that it would be a matter of course for him or her to undertake the care' - as the Ministry of Social Affairs describes it in its Guidelines - is eligible for the allowance. It is therefore not just for spouses, partners, children or parents, but for other people as well. It is therefore not an absolute condition that there should be a legal or blood relationship with the dying person. Neither is it necessary for the person in receipt of the allowance to live in the same house as the patient or even that the latter should be looked after in his or her own home. The allowance is, however, granted if the carer suffers a loss of income through undertaking the care. Spouses working at home, pensioners and social welfare recipients are therefore not eligible. The municipalities often have the means of providing other forms of financial assistance in these cases.

Under the new legislation also, a patient who chooses to end his/her days at home does not have to bear expenses which would be borne by the hospital if the patient were to be admitted. The cost of medicines and nursing materials are therefore also covered.

The guidelines on the project place much emphasis on information; people who undertake the caring should first be told what the illness will entail, what its course is likely to be and what help they are entitled to expect. They also emphasise that the existence of an allowance must not mean that friends and relatives feel pressurised into undertaking the care of a terminal patient at home. The patient, too, should not feel pressurised by the fact that an allowance may be available.

Experiences

The project is still so new that at the time of writing this casebook no evaluation research has as yet been carried out. A national newspaper, however, has examined a number of large municipalities in which ten per cent of Danes reside. Approximately one thousand people were found to have made use of the project.

Upon being asked, most of the local authorities expressed the opinion that it was a great success. The project has apparently saved the government large sums of money. In Århus - Denmark's second city -it was estimated that dying in a hospital bed cost twenty-four times as much as granting leave of absence to a family carer.

===
More information :
Ms. Hedvig Moller Larsen
Ribe County Council
Sorsigvej 35
DK-6760 Ribe
Tel: 75 42 42 00
===

4. France

SUPPORT GROUP FOR CARERS
The art is to be neither too involved nor too distant

There is a remarkable paradox about carers: everyone knows that their needs are very great, but they themselves think not. Is this because they do not know where they can get help? Has it something to do with the ties they have with their parents? In France, educationists, along with professionals and carers, went in search of a 'healthy' basis for family care. Their approach was to set up support groups in a course situation and then to research these thoroughly.

The initiative for the support groups came from a French institution, the Ecole des Parents et des Educateurs (EPE- The School for Parents and Educators). An institution of this nature which not only provides advice on education but also runs courses exists in a large number of French cities. The EPEs started support groups for carers in Paris, Metz, Marseilles and Bordeaux in 1988. This was not an easy task. The support group in Marseilles never really got going for lack of interest. In the other three cities, the carers also showed little interest. The hard core of the group in Paris remained restricted to four or five people, in Bordeaux six and in Metz ten. Nevertheless, the results from the support groups are worth while, especially since they were fairly systematically researched. Before embarking on the project some exploratory research was carried out into the experiences of other support groups in France. The Foundation de France (a private fund supporting social innovations) provided part of the funds, as did the Caisse National de Vieilesse (a pension scheme exploited by the French government) and two other pension funds.

What they provided
The support groups aim at adults who care for their fathers/mothers. The age of the participants varied from 45 to 65 years. One of the most important aims was preventing crises between children and parents. In this way escalations such as acts of violence and stopping the care could be limited. By making carers more conscience of the relationship carers have

with their parents they do not have to go to one of both extremes: either having too closely-knit a bond with the person (merging) or being too distant (rejecting).
In the support groups much attention is paid to the ageing process in combination with approaching death -not just the death of their parents, but also their own (Neizert, 1989).

In practical terms, the challenge was to help carers to combine succesfully their care of the elderly person with their own (family) life. To do so, they should not only see their own role clearly but also that of the elderly person; they should learn to recognise the limits to what they can do to help. It was important to re-establish or improve communications between those concerned: the carer, the parent(s) and the professional services. For this, the carers were trained in communicating and in dealing with everyday situations. The latter, not unimportant, aim was to inform and help carers to understand the mental and physical processes of getting older and approaching death. For this, they were not only given information (e.g. on ageing and Alzheimer's disease) but during the sessions the participants were also encouraged to speak freely about personal problems, conflicts and emotions.

Sessions

The support groups met ten times during a period varying from two and a half to ten months. The ten sessions each lasted between two and three hours.

From the start, the participants were aware that the group also served a scientific purpose. And this had its impact on the order of business. Each group had not only a group leader who was very well grounded in group dynamics but also an observer who acted, as it were, as the group's memory. It was his or her task to sum up each session. For this, two questions were posed at the beginning of each session: "What impressed you most the last time?" and "Has anything changed since last time in your relationship with your parent for whom you are caring?" This systematic approach helped the participants to keep a watch on their own development. The participants also had to fill in a detailed questionnaire in the first and last session.

The actual information was provided by external consultants: a gerontologist, a geriatrician, a psychiatrist, a psychologist or the manager of a day centre, for example.

Participants

Recruiting participants was done not only through social workers and the local media but also intensively by the EPE itself. Anyone who was caring for an older relative at home was eligible to take part. The only condition was that people would actually attend the sessions and were willing to cooperate in the research.
The participants had to pay anything except for a fifty Franc fee for compulsory membership of the EPE.

That altogether less than twenty participants out of such an enormous target group could be found shows how difficult it was to recruit people. This may be due to the fact that the EPEs have no suitable infrastructure for activities for the elderly. Their target group is usually considerably younger. Many practical reasons, also -such as the problem of replacing a carer temporarily- made recruitment more difficult.
But it appears that there were also psychological barriers to be overcome. Objectively speaking, carers may well be in great need of support, but subjectively this may be quite a different matter. Many of them, for example, have become used to the dependent position.

What it meant to carers

Even if recruitment was not easy, the participants themselves attached great importance to their support group. At last they were able unreservedly and without being judged to discuss all their problems. They also found the information very valuable since it helped to understand better the processes of ageing and dying. The support group also had a therapeutic effect on the personal relationships between the carer and the cared for parent as well as between other people. They were able to distance themselves better from their roles as carers.

A dual option

From the start, the EPE had two options. Not only to support the carers, but also to discover what was a 'healthy basis' for providing care. During

the research project, five aspects were therefore studied carefully:
- the image the carers had of old age;
- the relationship between the caring daughter or son and the father or mother;
- the context of that relationship (family, environment);
- the elderly person in question;
- the latter's view of the situation.

Keeping this dual option in mind, it may in any case be said that support groups are worth while, provided they are led by specially trained personnel. Through participating in the support groups, the carers began to see ageing in a new light, both in themselves and in the person for whom they were caring. The relationship between the elderly parent and the carer changed, mainly as a result of improved ways of communicating and because of better understanding. The carers learned to listen better, were more tolerant, felt more relaxed, took more pleasure in their work and assumed a better balanced attitude, both emotionally and psychologically, to the elder person.

At the end of the project, the carers had a clearer idea of the various positions within the houshold. Help from outside - whether or not from professionals - was accepted more easily and even appreciated. At the same time the support group helped the carers to escape from their isolation. The objective information they received on the medical and psychological aspects of caring helped them to adapt better to changings in their situation. Briefly, the carers seemed better able to bear their heavy burden.

The research report itself concludes with a fairly fundamental question: The aim was to offer support in the relationship between the helping child and the older parent, including the knowledge that this relationship is one day going to end. How far can one go? The caring child gets older, the elderly parent slowly declines. Is it not a bit on the late side for in-depth psychological interventions?

Recommendations for elsewhere

As we have said, it is only the carers who ignore that they really need help. Whether similar support groups can be set uo elsewhere is therefore very dependent upon whether the carers can be approached and their resistance overcome. Recruiting participants is still the greatest problem.

Once a support group has been put together, the combination of discussion and information provision will, according to the researchers, determine its success.

If the experiment is repeated, the support group - even if no research is involved - should be properly evaluated. There should also be an observer with the group, and the carers, too, should take part in the evaluation by completing questionnaires. In this way it will be possible to get a better idea of how the carers can be best supported, besides which this method encourages the carers to reflect upon their own situation.

Source:

Neitzert, Francoise, "Le soutien à la génération des 45-60 ans dans la rélation d'aide aux parents agés à domicile. Phase préliminaire", Fédération des Ecoles des Parents et des Educateurs (FNEPE) Juin 1989, Paris.

===
More information :
Ecole des parents et des educateurs
5 Impasse Bon Secours
F-75011 Paris
Tel: 43 48 00 16
===

5. Federal Republic of Germany

BERLIN SERVICE CENTRE PERFORMS PIONEER WORK FOR CARERS
The advantages of combining emotional support with practical support

From the 1970s onwards, the so-called 'Sozialstationen' began to appear in the Federal Republic of Germany. These were intended to bring together under one roof all the existing facilities and services for the elderly in each region. One of these service centres is in the Berlin district of Lichterfelde West. It has done pioneer work on behalf of carers.

The regionalisation of these services in one centre was not a sudden development. In the former West Germany the need for help was rapidly increasing, the local institutions (often connected with the Churches) were no longer able to cope and the costs had risen dramatically, particularly in respect to residential care. In Berlin, the operation of the new service centres was in the hands of the existing denominational institutions, as can be seen from their titles. For example the centre in Lichterfelde West is connected with the Evangelical Church. Its full title is 'Sozial/Diakoniestation Lichterfelde-west' (Social/Diaconate Centre for Lichterfelde West), usually abbreviated to DS.

In addition to health care in the home, all the service centres must provide counselling. However, they do not all offer exactly the same service but have their own specialisation. The Lichterfelde Centre specialises in supporting family carers.

Service provided
In 1990, a new Social Centre Act came into force in Berlin. In addition to health care in the home and counselling, the centres were required to include health promotion, prevention and rehabilitation. From then onwards, the support of family carers was part of the service centres' task. However, no extra funding was granted to cover this extra work. Neither was there sufficient qualified staff to do these extra jobs. At the time the Act came into force, the Lichterfelde Centre already had some experience in the support of carers. What kind of service were they providing? To begin with, district nursing: qualified nurses do not merely renew dressings and

give injections but they also wash patients. In addition, home help (from domestic work to cooking and help with finances) is part of the service.

The third ingredient in the package of services offered by Lichterfelde Centre is counselling. The centre's social workers advise people from their office (in 20%,) or at home (in 80% of the cases). This advice is mainly on social welfare or legal matters, but also on health. They also help people to fill in forms.

Support

Carers can go to the Centre for various kinds of support. They can take courses and join discussion groups, or present their questions and problems at individual counselling sessions. The courses for carers are held twice a year. For ten weeks at a time they meet in groups for one-and-a-half hours a week. The first few meetings are mainly on practical questions, after which problems of a more personal nature will be dealt with. The aim of the courses is roughly 'to be able to care without losing sight of oneself'.

The second type of support is the group discussions. The groups are mixed and participants include carers who look after the physically ill at home and those who care for people with psycho-geriatric problems. The carers of parents who have been admitted to hospital or have even died are also able to participate. The attendance at group discussions is usually very high. On average the carers only miss one session, in many cases because the care for the elderly must come first. This is in fact a problem in itself; sometimes participation in a discussion group may at first be an extra chore for the carer. It seems to help if the meetings are of a friendly nature; even carers do not object to being treated to tea and cake now and then.

The third form of support is the individual counselling sessions which are sometimes an extension of the discussion groups. The counselling is concerned with approaching personal problems but social and legal problems often also come up.

By taking part in these forms of support, the carers get a better idea of the current laws and regulations. They also develop self-confidence which may help them to feel less nervous of officials. Taking part in a group also helps carers to take important decisions; it also helps them to feel less guilty if, after all, the elderly person has to be admitted to an institution. The discussion groups also dispel feelings of loneliness and help carers to get over the death of the elderly person for whom they have been caring. The staff of Lichterfelde Centre endeavour to make the discussion groups become the basis for self-help groups. There are now plans to set up an association for carers.

Target group
The population of Lichterfelde West is around 25,000. At present, the Centre has 120 patients, 80% of whom are very elderly. These are usually disabled people and their relatives. The proportion of single women with psycho-geriatric problems is increasing, as is also the number of the chronically ill.

Generally speaking, three groups of carers make use of the Centre. The first are the caring partners, usually aged between 70 and 90. Often, they have no experience of support in a group; they usually take part for the first time after some crisis or on the advice of a doctor. The second group consists of caring daughters who are generally aged between 40 and 60. These women usually have some experience of groups. The third group consists of women (usually daughters) who can see that within a certain time they will be having to undertake the care of a family member.

Internal organisation
Almost forty people work at the Lichterfelde Centre. The active work is done by thirteen home helpers, 22 nurses (including one man) and two social workers. The social work is integrated as much as possible with the nursing service. The social workers often hear from colleagues from the Centre that there are problems occurring somewhere and then make house calls.

The other workers are mostly students who are intending to do this type of work in the future. But strictly speaking this does not increase the size of the staff since supervising students also takes up time.

The administrative work of the Centre is handled by two part-time to the Manager; the most recently appointed is a woman sociologist with some commercial training, whereas most service centres have a man with an economic background as manager. Until recently, the job of manager was also a voluntary one. The Centre receives a grant from the district of Berlin and is also funded by the health insurance funds, municipal schemes and other contributions. The elderly and their carers do not need to pay for the help they receive. The problem is, however, that the service centres cannot then claim for this help. Even after the Berlin 'Social Centres Act' no extra funds were forthcoming to aid carers. This means that since October 1991 the courses and group discussions are no longer free. The participants now pay DM 30 for the ten sessions.

The Centre is open Monday to Friday from 8 am to 7 pm. Outside these hours a message can be left on an answering machine. The service centres are now well-known in Berlin, both to the people themselves and to other bodies. Posters and leaflets at chemists', doctors' surgeries and other official services help to make carers aware of the existence of support. The service is also made known to a wider public through the press.

Cooperation

Cooperation with intramural bodies is varied. There is an excellent relationship with the Psycho-geriatric Department of the Free University; there is an interchange of students and the University clinic offers beds to sufferers from dementia over the age of 60. Collaboration is not so fruitful with the nearest hospital. Here, because of cost, chronic patients are discharged as quickly as possible, which often means they have to go home, putting a lot of pressure on their carers. There is quite good cooperation from the social workers at the hospital, as long as there are personal contacts. The Centre has been able to make satisfactory and practical arrangements with the GPs in their area. Against this, the health insurance funds can be difficult. Each fund has its own – often incomprehensible – forms. The funds are statutorily obliged to advise their policy holders but this does not always happen. They also want people to attend in person at their office, even those who are seriously ill. This means that it takes a long time for the request to be dealt with; at present there is a two-month delay.

find that the officials are not friendly disposed to them. For many, this raises such a barrier that they just do not make use of local government benefits to which they are entitled.

Experiences

The fact that support for carers is integrated at a service centre and not independently organised has many advantages. The service centres are well known and have ties with the local people, in the case of Lichterfelde West through the three Evangelical churches in the area. Those working in the centre are familiar with the home circumstances of many local people.
The integration also means that the service provided is wider-ranging and more versatile; care and support for carers form an organic whole.

However, there are problems too. More capacity is required to provide support for carers, but the means and the time are lacking. The social workers at the Centre also feel they are underpaid. They themselves blame this on the fact that theirs has always been regarded as women's work.

The support of carers is a form of service which is still developing. This means, among other things, that much attention must be paid to the training of new people. The presence of students ought not to hinder the group processes, and this is sometimes a problem. There ought also to be more exchanges between the various workers in the field. Fortunately, in Berlin a Carers' working group for this purpose has been in existence for several years now.

===
More information :
Marion Rohn-Kronbach
Sozialstation - Diakoniestation
Berlin - Lichterfelde - West
Hindenburgdamm 101A
D-1000 Berlin 45
Tel: 030 8344365/5091
===

6. Federal Republic of Germany

ADVICE BUREAU FOR CARERS
Keeping emotional support separate from practical help

A terraced house in the northern German town of Norderstedt - a suburb of Hamburg - is home to the Medical Advice Bureau for the Elderly and their Carers. Three female employees sit in a livingroom-like atmosphere, ready to advise those who take care of elderly relatives in their own homes.

The first objective is to offer emotional support. Practical help is not offered because this might lead to ambiguities. Anyone coming with a request for practical help will be referred.

The advice bureau has been running for a number of years now. In 1981 it emerged as the result of research which the University of Hamburg had begun as far back as 1977. The research project is now complete but since 1987 the advice bureau has been able to continue on the strength of a government grant.

The title of 'Medical Advice Bureau' is a little confusing. It suggests that only medical advice is available. The reason for this choice of title was because people come more readily for advice to a medical rather than a non-medical service. Furthermore, the chosen title conveys the notion that the bureau is concerned with medical care.

Emotional support

What has the 'medical' advice bureau to offer? First and foremost, of course, advice to carers. But in addition the bureau also provides training and supervision for both professional and voluntary workers in the care of the elderly. The bureau staff receive telephone calls from all over Germany enquiring, among other things, about how to set up a similar service elsewhere in the country. The Norderstedt Advice Bureau has been running for years and has been thoroughly researched; it enjoys a wide reputation and acts as an example.

However, its main function is to advise carers. The staff give their advice in individual interviews, meetings with the family and services caring for the elderly and at support groups for carers. The advice is chiefly concerned with factual information on care. This is very often linked with advice on death and bereavement, and solicitude. Thirdly, they are regularly asked for advice regarding personality disturbances or difficulties in the relations between the carer and elderly person cared for. The research worker from Hamburg University concluded that "Such support makes sense only if there is a strong and obvious will to look after the elderly person with dedication in the family home."

The individual interviews - which usually take place as the result of a telephone call from the carer - are where possible held at first in the home of the carer but then preferably at the Advice Bureau.

Target group
By far the major part of the advice bureau's work is for carers and to a lesser extent for the elderly people concerned. Most of the bureau's clients are daughters or daughters-in-law between the ages of forty and sixty who are looking after their mothers or mothers-in-law. Male carers seldom consult the bureau. The same applies to husbands looking after their wives.

The ages of the elderly being cared for is from 55 to 90. Those who come for advice to the bureau mainly belong to the middle class. Those in the upper class obviously have other ways. The poor are less easily accessible but this also applies to other facilities in the Federal Republic.

The carers usually make their first contact with the bureau by telephone. It may also happen that their children take the initiative since they see the pressure upon their mother as a threat to the family.

Carers who come to the bureau are often going through a crisis at that time. They are sometimes on the brink of nervous exhaustion, for example because the elderly person has to go into hospital or a nursing home. It is rare that a carer gets in touch with the bureau as a precautionary measure. Usually some problem to do with the physical condition of the patient is the reason for the enquiry. Often carers have been given high expectations by the doctors in charge and then been disappointed. They then expect the advice bureau to tell them what they want to hear. And there, too, their hopes will usually be dashed.

Disillusionment
As well as individual counselling and discussions with families in which a dementia sufferer is being cared for, the advice bureau also offers carers an opportunity to take part in support groups. In 1987 the federal state of Schleswig-Holstein (to which Norderstedt belongs) to start a pilot project in this field. Support groups of this type would be set up in five locations. The five staff members of the first advice bureau were given the task of setting up a like number of support groups. Each of them became the group leader; in some places an assistant group leader was added. The support groups ran for quite some time; in three locations they have become part of the regular service.

The advice bureau staff estimate that a carer needs to be part of a support group for about two years in order to find the solution to her/his problem. After this, they can detach themselves from the 'bosom' of the group.

The support groups often first have the job of crisis intervention. After this they usually look back in order to arrive at a realistic and balanced view of the generation problem and the care. Both in individual interviews and in the groups, the advice carers receive is often disillusioning at first. In the early stages the conflicts are the severest. Later on the advice bureau staff work towards the personal development and personal maturity of the carer in her relations with the elderly person. Only on this basis is it possible, moreover, to overcome the problems which they encounter every day in their care. This maturing is also aimed at helping them to make difficult decisions, such as allowing the elderly person eventually to go into a nursing home. The University of Hamburg researcher's conclusion here was: 'The family very often becomes so exhausted that admission is the sensible thing. It is often even necessary in order to avoid the total breakdown of the mother-child relationship during the difficult final stage of care. The support is aimed at giving intensive counselling in respect of such a decision and helping the carer to feel that it is legitimate, after so much effort in the home, to consider letting the patient go into professional care.' The job situation of the carers is seldom brought to the advice bureau as a problem. This may be because most of the clients are housewives or women who had earlier given up their jobs to care for an older person.

Internal organisation
After Hamburg University had completed their research project, the municipality of Norderstedt, the district of Segeberg and the federal state of Schleswig-Holstein each undertook to pay one-third of the costs of running the service. The amount is fixed annually and in 1991 the total exceeded 215,000 marks. One of the conditions for grant aid is that the advice bureau makes it clear how much need exists for its services. It must also keep on organising training courses. The clients do not have to pay anything.

The staff of the advice bureau - a psychologist, a professional carer of the elderly and an administrative assistant - work as a closely-knit team. There is no strict division of labour since all three have training in the therapeutic and counselling work. The advice bureau is pleased about this. In this work it does not matter what professional background the employees have, as long as they have plenty of experience in working with the elderly and are aware of the kind of problems which may occur between them and their carers. Therapeutic experience is also a considerable advantage here.

The head of the advice bureau is a doctor but the latter is not involved in the daily therapeutic and counselling work. He acts as supervisor and negotiates, for example, with the providers of funds. There are no voluntary workers at the bureau.

The area served by the bureau is the town of Norderstedt in the federal state of Schleswig- Holstein. In this same state there is also an advice bureau in the city of Kiel. Another is at present being set up in Flensburg.

The most recent statistics for the Norderstedt bureau date from 1989. In that year over five hundred counselling telephone calls were made, lasting for maximum one hour (calls lasting for less than five minutes are not included). The staff also conducted 415 personal counselling sessions and made 78 house calls. The reason why so much counselling is done on the telephone is because there are only three advice bureaux in the federal state (which has over 2.5 million inhabitants, 16% of whom are over 65). Although exact figures are not available, the impression given is that more and more enquiries are coming in to the bureau. Doctors and 'Sozialstationen' (service centres for the elderly) are referring more often, and carers themselves are also finding it easier to approach the bureau.

Experiences

The advice bureau in Norderstedt works independently. This is not absolutely essential. It could very well have closer links with the Sozialstationen. It has, however, excellent relations with the latter and with the residential homes in the region, especially since its staff organise the training courses and supervision. They would like to have closer contacts with the general practitioners and consultants. The care provided within the region has now - since the bureau reported some discrepancies - been extended to include short stays in care; there are also plans for a day care centre.

The advice bureau has demonstrated its value. At first this became clear when the results were scientifically measured. Now it is demonstrated by the fact that the carers go through life with lighter burdens. They have become convinced that they have done whatever they could and that is more important than the question whether they have kept up the care 'right up to the end' or whether they could have prevented the elderly person from having to be admitted to hospital or a home. According to the researcher from the University of Hamburg, this understanding will also have an impact on their own life expectancy.

From the clients' point of view, the advice bureau does not give enough counselling in the matter of practical care. The carers also feel it is a pity the advice they receive does not immediately get results and that the staff cannot give them ready-made recipes for success. This is, however, not their intention. Hospitals and other institutions exist for the nursing. They actually try to avoid the practical side becoming entangled with the emotional, as might happen if one and the same person offered both. The danger would then be that problems requiring support on the emotional plane would be concealed and ignored due to the fact that one is concentrating on the practical problems.

===
More information :
Dr. Jens Bruder
Ärztliche Beratungsstelle für ältere Menschen und ihre Angehöringen
Rüsternweg 26a
D-2000 Norderstedt
Tel: 040 5254011
===

7. Greece

HELP AT HOME

Four years ago, the municipal authority of Argyroupolis - a suburb near Athens inhabited by a relatively large number of people with an average income - took a far-reaching decision. 'Help at home' must be provided from then on: social, medical and practical help, for families who were having problems of some kind. This decision was far-reaching because the Greek government had made no financial provision for this new service although it had earlier approved it. Elsewhere in Greece this was a reason to give up projects of this nature. In Argyroupolis, however, 'Help at Home' became a political priority.[3]

Service provided

'Help at Home' is intended to support people who live at home and are dependent on the help of others. The majority are elderly; of the 120 people who make use of the service, only ten are under the age of 55 and they are chronically ill.

The service offers, firstly, domestic help such as cleaning, shopping, cooking and help with bathing. In addition, medical help can be supplied such as doctors' visits, medicines, physiotherapy and nursing. Lastly it includes help for people to function socially by means of social work - both for the elderly and for the carers - voluntary work and activities.

A regular check is made to ascertain whether people need 'Help at Home' and, if so, how much and how often. There is, however, no time limit.

The project was preceded by a limited research. Twelve sociology students conducted a house-to-house survey of the welfare situation of families in Argyroupolis. This produced a list of 350 families who were having problems. The project social worker was then able to find out the extent

---

[3] After the first year the Third EC Proverty Programme came to the rescue.

of their need. Finally the project started off with fifty families. Some of the selection criteria were whether the user could look after himself/herself, whether there were family members who could help him or her and whether there were financial problems.

The project was publicised through advertisements and broadcasts on local radio. At the beginning of the project an intensive media campaign was organised. This was repeated at the end of 1991. At present there are plans to make a video which would help to make the project more widely known.

Internal organisation
The project committee is broadly based. In addition to local authority representatives and the coordinator of the poverty programme, there are members of EOMMEX (an organisation for small traders), the OAED (a national employment organisation) and of the voluntary organisations.

'Help at Home' works with a modest staff quota. There is a coordinator who is permanently employed with the local authority but seconded to the project. Then there is a social worker (who, along with the coordinator, represents the driving force behind the project), a doctor who pays an average of three calls a day, one district nurse, one physiotherapist, one home help and one driver who not only drives for the staff but also transports the clients. Most of these workers are part-time. They are very dedicated ("This is not just any old work") although they - like everyone else in the social sector in Greece - are paid badly and have to work under conditions which are not ideal.

Even when the number of families availing of the Help at Home service grew from 50 to 120 within one year, this small staff was adequate. There is, however, a need for one more nurse who could help with bathing the elderly. The project is still attracting new users and the demand is growing. An estimated quarter of the population of Argyroupolis are over the age of sixty. About five per cent, i.e. 350 people, qualify for Help at Home. This means that only one-third of the potential clientele are actually receiving help now.

The project collaborates closely with the local hospitals. When a patient is being discharged from hospital, Help at Home will be informed, even if the person has never used this service before. There is also close cooperation with the two local open centres for the elderly - or KAPIs, as they are called. The elderly using the Help at Home service is also entitled to take part in the KAPI activities, such as day trips, camping holidays and parties. This is particularly important to the carers since it can afford a short respite for them. Cooperation with the local homes for the elderly is a lot more difficult. The Help at Home staff feel that the quality of these homes is inferior and they are too expensive. They would only refer people to them in an emergency.

Payment
Any resident of Argyroupolis can make use of Help at Home services; these are free. One of the selection criteria is, however, that the applicant must not be financially well-off. The appreciation people have for 'Help at Home' has not been systematically examined but according to the staff, those who make use of it are 'extremely grateful'. It is interesting to note that some of the carers appreciated the services so much that they wanted to pay for them. The staff would not take this money. Anyone who feels this is strange should realise that the Greeks make a clear distinction between free and privately paid-for services. Income-related payments are hardly even considered.

Residential care alternatives
One of the problems Help at Home encountered was that a good many families wanted them to find a permanent or temporary place in a residential home for the elderly person for whom they were caring. The staff had to keep on encouraging people to retain responsibility for the care themselves and give them the necessary support. This took a lot of time but was considered important; after all, a place in a home costs a great deal and the care provided is mediocre.

A second problem was that many of the elderly felt they were under pressure from their families when it came to the question of property or inheritances. Some of the elderly has transferred ownership of their property to their children in the expectation that they would then look after them. This, however, made them more vulnerable and helpless. This illustrates the darker side of care; sometimes children refuse to look after their parents, take no responsibility at all or else even abuse them. "It is sometimes necessary to explain that older people may act a little strangely. Their children are not trained to cope with them but our social worker can advise them in such cases," says one of the staff members.

The third problem is linked to this. Carers in Argyroupolis - which as already mentioned is a new area - find it more difficult to take their problems to other members of the family or to neighbours than would be the case in some of the older districts of Athens, for example. In these older communities the men would often sit in the cafés and the women would know their neighbours better. In addition, there were inexpensive restaurants there where single people could eat and small local shops which served as meeting-places and information centres. New areas thus demand new services. The local authorities recognise this fact; there is already a plan for a 'meals-on-wheels' service which will eventually be run by local people who are unemployed or in receipt of disability benefits.

Help at Home would like to involve the local community, especially as voluntary workers. At present six or seven voluntary workers are helping but, generally speaking, their contribution is not really very useful. This may have something to do with the lack of a long tradition of organised voluntary work which, apart from the Christian tradition of philanthropy and charity which is particularly evident in such organisations as the Red Cross, YWCA and the active church groups. In areas such as Argyroupolis there is a lack of any form of spontaneous voluntary work, without organised networks filling this gap.

Recommendations
In Greece there is also an obvious need for local projects such at Help at Home. Many local authorities realise this, but are fraustrated by the government, which imposes restrictions. Moreover they do not have the means to realise their plans and they give them too low a priority. The EC can play a crucial role in such local areas by funding pilot projects. This will also provide practical examples. Although the EC has helped to

fund the Argyroupolis project, the local authority representatives chosen are those who feel that social services are a priority. They have also proved expert in finding alternative financial resources for the benefit of the whole community.

What is interesting in the Greek project is the cooperation between the various sections of the public sector: the small traders' organisation, the employment exchange, centres for the elderly, hospitals, local government, voluntary organisations and education services. This pluralistic approach is badly needed in Greece since the local authorities there cannot possibly bear the burden of all the social services. Indeed, because they fear that they will be left to fund these on their own, some local authorities refuse to move into this field at all. When setting up home care programmes, municipalities will have to be creative in finding new forms of cooperation with a whole range of public services, private organisations, volunteer organisations and individuals.

===
More information :
"Help at Home"
Municipality of Argyropoulis
Konstantinopoulos 83
GR-Argyropoulis 164 52
===

8. Italy

COMUNITÀ S. EGIDIO
Professionals in voluntary work

ACAP, an organisation associated with the Roman Catholic church which helps the elderly in their homes, has been in existence in Rome for almost twenty years. A short time ago ACAP also started a residential group for the elderly. It is characteristic of the political relations in Italy similar initiatives, which are associated with the socialist party, exist in other districts of Rome. According to the people who work for ACAP these private organisations are more flexible than the public organisations. At least they existed before there were public organisations.

When ACAP started in 1973, Italian government hardly offered any home care. Even worse, public discussion of this need had hardly even got going. For the elderly on minimum incomes, who were ill or isolated, there was no alternative but to go into hospital. The result was that there was much suffering and misery among this group of old people in certain areas of Rome. If the elderly were finally admitted to hospital they soon became the victims of hospitalisation. They became less independent every day, their health deteriorated and they sometimes even died unnecessarily.

In order to change this situation, the ACAP took the initiative of setting up a kind of health service which would enable the elderly to remain living in their own homes. Pilot projects had not yet come into existence; the first official municipal caring project did not begin until 1979 and by the time the first steps were taken to obtain legislation governing this kind of facility, ACAP had been running for quite a while. It is not surprising, therefore, that ACAP's pioneer work was on a fairly pragmatic basis.

Service provided
What is it that the ACAP people do? Individual care, to begin with; helping people with getting up and going to bed, washing, dressing, keeping an eye on their nutrition and accompanying them to the doctor. Nursing - including therapy, emergency aid, tests - and help with rehabilitation are part of the ACAP package. Special attention is paid to the latter: good posture,

help in using orthopaedic equipment, speech therapy and adaptations to the home.
As well as personal care, the ACAP service also covers domestic chores like cleaning, or dealing with the plumber or electrician. In addition, they encourage people to undertake all kinds of jobs themselves, from cooking their own food and reading the newspaper to shopping and going for walks. The ACAP people stay with the dying, too, during their final hours. Certain kinds of social work are undertaken, like helping with correspondence, fetching their pensions and finding out about the various official bodies in the community.

Part of this social service is supporting the family circle of which the elderly person is a part. If necessary the ACAP workers try to solve problems other family members may have with money, work or housing. This fits in with the objective of the project which is to maintain the elderly for as long as possible in their own domestic environment. The main aim of these activities is to prevent the person from being sent to hospital. Instead, it is preferable to improve the quality of his or her life. If the person is under treatment or convalescing, ACAP will provide support in this situation. The starting point is always the individual situation of the elderly person himself or herself. A plan of care is then drawn up, tailored to his or her requirements and adjusted in the course of time as changes occur. The help of ACAP is directly meant for the elderly themselves, who need care at home. It is meant for carers only in the second place. But of course they profit by the efforts of the organisation. If a carer indicates that he or she can not cope any more, the ACAP will stand in.

Scope
By 1986, ACAP was providing a service in eleven districts of Rome to more than a thousand people. Over half of these were cared for at home. Over five hundred elderly people were taking part in activities at six day centres throughout the city. During one randomly-selected week, ten ACAP workers made 130 journeys with elderly people either to hospital or to a nursing home.

ACAP is best known from hearsay publicity. Moreover, most professionals and people living in the district know of its existence, so that the elderly too are told to go to them. Its address and telephone number are regularly printed in the newspapers.

The ACAP service is for any elderly person threatened with hospitalisation. It is therefore for people who do not attend - or at any rate have great difficulty in getting to - the normal facilities, either because these do not exist in their area or because their income is just over the limit up to which they are entitled to free medical care. These may well be people who live in poor circumstances and are suffering from loneliness, often due to problems within the family. They are usually the chronically ill older elderly for whom the prognosis is poor.

A random sample of 45 elderly people showed that the majority (38) were women. Many of them can still look after themselves to a large extent; only eight of them lived with their families. The majority of old people using ACAP's services are between the ages of 66 and 75 or are over 85. The amount of attention they receive from ACAP depends upon their living conditions. If they are old people who are mainly independent, someone will spend one hour a week with them. The same applies to those who live with other people on whom they can call for help. ACAP organises a two-hour meeting twice a week for this fairly active group.

For the elderly who cannot manage on their own, the service varies from three hours a week (for those who have some other form of help in the home) to one or two hours a day. If an emergency arises - for example the elderly person may fall ill and be taken to the hospital - help can even be provided on a 24-hour basis. All these forms of assistance are provided by various professional groups who are attached to ACAP, i.e. social workers, workers with the elderly, physiotherapists, GPs, consultants, nurses and dietitians.

Residential group
Since 1979, ACAP is also in charge of a residential group for the elderly on a similar basis. At that time the problem was to find something for three elderly people who were being cared for at home by ACAP but would have had to go to hospital if no alternative had been created. The elderly on low incomes cannot, in any case, afford a bed in a nursing or

residential home in Italy, so the only answer is to go into a hospital ward. Since that time the residential group has included elderly people who have very little money and who are hardly able, if at all, to look after themselves. At first elderly people who were partly able to look after themselves were sometimes accepted, but gradually the criteria have become more stringent.

The apartments have been adapted for the elderly; the bathrooms and passageways have supports and handrails and the beds are high enough. The demands made on the elderly are geared to their limited abilities; they do not have to help each other neither do they have to share their facilities with anyone else. They can bring their own furniture. At present there are eighteen elderly people in residence.

Funding
ACAP is not receiving structural subsidy, but exists on tax-exempt private donations and legacies. The church donates money too and government gives financial support per project. Parents themselves are the last source of income. However, funding is a permanent problem the ACAP has to cope with. All ACAP employees are on the payroll, except for the doctor, who volunteers a number of hours a week. His main task is advising ACAP employees. Besides, there is a large number of volunteers involved with ACAP. Volunteers, for instance, work in the commune in three shifts of three to five people. The kind of services they offer, consist for the greater part of personal and domestic care, assisting with forms etc., but they also keep people company and work with groups.

Recommendations
The work of ACAP does not provide a universal model. It has been built up from experience closely linked to certain districts of Rome itself. The initiators themselves are, however, most enthusiastic because they claim their work is very original, an 'expression of social creativity' which may inspire others. But merely copying their initiative in order to save money, would not, they feel, make sense.

ACAP asks the elderly for an income-related contribution and does not give help to elderly people who earn more than a million lire a month. In doing so the ACAP consciously chooses to give priority to the poor and disabled.

Especially in countries where there is no developed welfare state, this priority regulation is sheer necessity according to the people of ACAP.

==
More information :
"Comunità S. Egidio"
Piazza S. Egidio 3A
I-00153 Rome
Tel: 06 5895945/5803548
==

9. The Netherlands

HELPING DEMENTIA PATIENTS AND THEIR CARERS - A study course
Beginning with the professionals in the interests of the carers

On average, people are living longer and longer and the realisation is growing that nursing homes and other institutions are not the ideal places for them to live in. The combination of these two factors has presented professional home carers with new problems. For example, more serious psycho-geriatric problems, but also the challenge of working with non-professionals to provide suitable care for elderly people. In order to train the professional carers for this, the Nijmegen Institute for Social Medicine and the Nijmegen University Institute of General Practitioners have developed a course. This course was first given in 1985, after which it went all over the country. And this, too, has been a success.

Proper supervision of dementia sufferers living at home and those around them demands a great deal of the professional carers. They not only need to know the symptoms of dementia and how to deal with it, but also what are the problems facing family carers and what facilities there are, in spite of these, for caring for patients at home.

The course had therefore three definite objectives. Firstly, to allow carers to gain some insight into the problems which dementia sufferers and those around them encounter every day. Then the carers were shown what practical facilities existed for relieving the burden of care at home. And finally they had to learn how not to act alone but **together with** the elderly person and the carers to make the best of the situation.

Internal organisation

The course was designed in the context of scientific research on the subject of "the elderly with behavioural disturbances and their social environment" which was begun in Nijmegen in 1984. The main question to be answered by this research was whether specific support for the carers could improve the situation of the elderly and of the carers, or at lease stabilise it. In addition, there was the question as to whether such support would lead to a reduction in the number of admissions to nursing homes and rest homes.

One source of funding for this research was the Prevention Fund. This is a national institution which subsidises research into ways of preventing health disorders. The Prevention Fund suggested to the researchers not to restrict themselves to a theoretical approach alone but to try immediately to find practical means. This became the course of study. It was thus not only a means by which to answer the question posed by the research project but resulted in something of practical value to others.

The students
In order to recruit researchers-cum-students, the care organisations in the Nijmegen area were directly approached. Here, people were immediately enthusiastic; support for family carers was felt to be one of the main tasks of the professional carers but a suitable form of support was still being sought. The professional family carers and workers with the elderly were allowed to take the course during working hours. The researchers bore the other expenses; the family care organisation did not have to pay any extra for the course. A maximum of fifteen students could take it at one time.

When the course was first provided in 1985 the only professionals selected for participation were those working in family care and the care of the elderly. This was because the organisers were convinced that only these workers had been long enough in the client's home to fulfil their supportive role unobtrusively.

Supervision
The course lasted ten months and began with a meeting on two consecutive days. This was found to be most useful; it gave the students a basis and helped them to get to know each other. After the two initial days the students just went on with their work. In the succeeding months they came together once every five weeks for a meeting lasting about two hours. This was partly for the transfer of information and partly to give practical guidance.

Halfway through the course, this method was found to be a little too abstract. The organisers then changed the order of the programme, making the students' own practical experiences the starting point for the lectures.

In the period between the meetings the participants received five hours of supervision per carer from their tutors. During this period they could also get in touch by telephone with the researchers at the Institute of Social Medicine. Since the course was mainly of significance to the researchers in the context of their research, they did not organise it a second time. They did, however, produce a handbook entitled 'Caring for elderly dementia sufferers at home' for the use of anyone who wished to set up a similar course elsewhere. Two thousand copies of this handbook were printed and it is now on its second edition. In view of the smallness of the Dutch market, this is an indication that there is a very big demand for methods by which to give carers systematic support. The number of symposia and conferences at which the researchers were invited to speak is also an indication of this demand.

The course was initially designed for those caring for families and the elderly but it would appear to be suitable for the training of other target groups. In the first instance these could include general practitioners, district nurses and district carers of the sick. But in Amsterdam a family care organisation has been offering a slightly adapted form of the course to voluntary workers as well.

Experiences and problems
During the course when it was first given in Nijmegen it was found that family carers had difficulty in keeping a certain distance between themselves and the elderly person and carer. Even the professionals usually showed a greater tendency to become too involved than to remain truly detached.

The students also had great difficulty in not taking sides, whether for the elderly person or for the carer. Here it becomes evident that those who attempt to support the carers always serve two clients who each have their own interests. The art of the professional is to steer an independent course between the two; neither side will benefit if a professional worker takes the side of one of them.

In its original form the course lasted ten months. This was found to be a workable period even though it could certainly be given over a shorter period. The advantage is that the theory takes better root if there is a period of not more than two or three weeks between the meetings; the students can then obtain practical experience in a more systematic manner. The actual planning, however, depends to some extent on the institution for which the students work.

What it means to the carers
The course was primarily targeted at the professional workers themselves; those providing family care and working with the elderly. But it also means something for the voluntary carers; they will obviously benefit if the professionals are better able to cope with 'their' elderly person and are also able to regard the carers as their partners in this task.

The Nijmegen research project highlighted the impact of this support in a rather unexpected way. It was found, strangely enough, not to be very effective where male carers were concerned. This may be because the support is intended to help carers to go about their tasks in a more businesslike way. Men had obviously learned to do this already.

It was also found that, for female carers who did not live with the elderly person, this direct support was actually counterproductive. The explanation for this may be that the effect of this support made them increase their efforts but that, by doing so, they had too little time for themselves. The support was, however, successful in preventing further admissions to institutions.

Fortunately, the support was of benefit to most of the carers. It helped them to cope better with their work and to feel greater satisfaction.

The second part of the research question - "does supporting the carers limit the numbers of admissions?" - also produced a positive conclusion; especially when the carer was not the partner, fewer people were admitted to a nursing or rest home than was the case in a comparable control group.

Recommendations for elsewhere

The research showed that it was quite possible, via direct support, to help carers to cope better with their work so that those for whom they were caring could remain longer in their own homes. The course was a feasible way in which to achieve this. It is a course which also seems fairly simple to transfer to another location (even though exact figures are not available for this, apart from the number of handbooks published). It is therefore worthwhile setting up similar courses in other parts of Europe.

A few points should be noted in this connection, however. Firstly that the students seemed to appreciate very much the combination of practice and theory it afforded. The transfer of knowledge on its own is not enough but this also applies to limiting the discussion to people's own experiences.
The second point is that support seems to be particularly effective if it is given unobtrusively. This makes the target group of professional carers such an ideal instrument; they can use their practical support as the entrée to providing emotional support as well.

The research results also sound a warning note: not all groups of carers appear to benefit equally from direct support by the professionals. Thus, in other parts of Europe one should also use this type of support selectively.

Finally, even the professionals needed constant supervision during this course. It is obviously not at all a simple matter for them to support voluntary carers without falling into the classic role of taking over part of the care and keeping it under their control. Carers might well benefit more from a limited number of hours of support by a well-trained professional than from a large number of hours from one who is not really au fait with the situation.

===
More information :
Mw. M. Vernooij
Instituut voor Huisarts-, Verpleeghuis- en Sociale Geneeskunde
Postbus 9101
NL-6500 HB Nijmegen
===

10. The Netherlands

TEMPORARY HELP VIA A CALL-IN CENTRE
Voluntary workers are not an extension of professional care

All too often people caring for a dementia sufferer in her/his own home need temporary help, after which they can again manage alone. But this kind of temporary help is particularly difficult to find, even in the Netherlands, with all its services. In Schiedam, a city in the densely-populated western part of the country, they have found a fairly simple solution to this problem: a call-in centre for voluntary workers.

The partners or other carers of the elderly living at home who have psycho-geriatric problems, or professional carers, just have to make their needs known. The call-in centre then finds someone who could come in to help for a few hours on a regular basis. The carer can then get out for a while even if only to go to the hairdresser or shops.

Service provided
The centre's volunteers offer themselves in the first place as sitters-in, usually for one or two mornings or afternoons a week. They can also fill in for whole days if they are free. One condition is that the elderly person must be known to the social/geriatric services of RIAGG (the Regional Institute for Mental Health Care). At the beginning it was only the partners of dementia sufferers who were eligible for this voluntary help. But in the course of time help was also offered to the carers of dementia patients who lived under the same roof. The (voluntary) carers of these patients who do not live with them may also have their load lightened from time to time.

The support provided by the volunteers in practice covers more than just being in the house. Not only because the volunteer wants to keep the elderly person occupied in as pleasant a way as possible but because he or she in many cases offers the carer a listening ear. In this way, the volunteer provides emotional support.

The periods of voluntary help vary greatly. Sometimes the situation deteriorates so rapidly that the elderly person may have to be admitted to an institution after only a few weeks. But in other cases the volunteer may pay regular visits to the elderly person for as long as eighteen months.

Until recently, carers could only call the Centre during the day. Since October 1991, however, there is also a night service. It was found that there was a growing need for the reassuring presence of a volunteer during the night hours. It is just during these hours that dementia patients are often very restless, so that the carer runs the risk of becoming exhausted. The volunteer who comes to take night duty stays from ten in the evening until eight in the morning and may also help during this time with simple jobs like dressing, toileting and preparing breakfast.

The night service is not only available for the elderly with psycho-geriatric problems but also for those who are just out of hospital and are fearful of being on their own. The carers of those who have been ill for a long time or of the disabled may also apply for help.

Internal organisation
The Call-in Centre came into existence when, in the mid-1980s, helpers and carers realised there were gaps in the support provided to people with psycho-geriatric problems. There was an especially great need for help on a temporary basis with the lighter tasks. It was anticipated that if such help were provided, there would be less likely to be a demand for help with the heavier duties.

Contact was established with the local authorities in Schiedam who, in 1988 and 1989, supervised the running of the Centre and grant-aided it on an experimental basis. The experiment led to an extension of this new form of service to the whole region, which has a population of almost 200,000. Subsidies were requested from the other local authorities as well; however, these have so far not been forthcoming.

The two coordinators and a project manager are paid out of the grant. The coordinators are each responsible for the day-to-day running of the service in part of the area served. The overall responsibility devolves on the project manager who is also head of the paramedical service at one of the local nursing homes. The grant also covers the volunteers' insurance and expenses. The carers themselves do not have to pay anything.

A Management Committee was set up to formulate general policy. This includes representatives of RIAGG and the organisation of social workers. There is also regular contact with other primary health care services and voluntary organisations. The coordinator and project manager are employed by the two nursing homes who run the Call-in Centre. They recruit and guide the volunteers, handle the incoming requests from carers, supply information to others and look after the project's finances.

Most of the carers have been made aware of the service by RIAGG. The aim is that general practitioners and professional carers, too, should make them aware of the Centre's existence. In this way it is easier to supply voluntary help first so that more intensive, professional help may not be required until a later stage.

The carers themselves do not lightly make use of the Centre. There is obviously still some kind of taboo operating here; they want to go on managing as long as they can by themselves. Often carers would prefer to have professional help; you don't have to feel so grateful for this.

As soon as a professional helper or carer makes a request to the Centre, the latter makes contact with RIAGG. This institute supplies the necessary information on the prognosis and situation of the elderly person. But in addition someone from the Centre, usually the coordinator and a volunteer, will also make a house call. They assess how much help is needed and which of the volunteers would be the most suitable to send.

The volunteers
Most of the volunteers are women, usually between the ages of 45 and 60. In recent times, men have also begun to come forward. This is good, since the elderly and the carers often ask for a male volunteer. As far as education and background are concerned, the volunteers are fairly mixed.

Once every two months the volunteers meet. At such contact meetings they can discuss their experiences and exchange helpful hints. The work demands a great deal of the volunteers. They have to be flexible, have time and patience to spare, but also a good deal of experience of life. Great emotional demands are made upon them while at the same time it is often difficult to make satisfactory contact with the elderly dementia sufferers.

This is why a lot of energy is expended on guidance and training. An information booklet has also been compiled.

In view of the heavy responsibility of the task, there is also some selection of applicants. Most volunteers offer of their own accord, having read something about the Centre in the newspaper. If the coordinator does not feel the candidate is yet suitable, a short period of voluntary work in one of the nursing homes is often a useful transition exercise. Candidates who are immediately suitable first attend a contact meeting of volunteers and then a two-day training session.

Both the requests for help and the volunteers may come from anywhere in the region. In 1990 there were 21 volunteers active in Schiedam and the surrounding area, calling to a total of 32 addresses.

Publicity
The staff of the Call-in Centre have given constant attention to publicity. This is achieved, among other ways, by giving out information to people and institutions who have anything to do with dementia patients. The local newspapers also give space - at the Centre's request - to the volunteer project through press releases and interviews. The latter in particular seem to evoke many reactions. The fact that the Centre was one of the first projects in this field has certainly contributed to the interest taken by the national newspapers in it on a number of occasions.

Experiences and recommendations
Voluntary work must be regarded as a special kind of work. It is complementary to self-care on the one hand and to professional care on the other. Its special nature must be emphasised, in the opinion of the Call-in Centre staff. This particular type of volunteer evolved only after it was realised that there were gaps in the care already provided; it is not there to fill in for the professionals. The carers themselves are very enthusiastic about the services given by the Centre. "Thanks to having a volunteer to come in I can now go back to choir practice each week" and "Now I don't have to hurry so much over the shopping; I am finding it easier all the time to stay out a bit longer". They seemed to have far more complaints about the professional services; they were patchy, passive,

impersonal and there were too many changes of staff. By contrast, they appreciated the continuity and personal character of the volunteers' services all the more.

The carers also appreciate very much the contact they have with the volunteers; it helps them a lot. In this respect the Centre not only provides a good complementary service to the work of the professionals, but also to that of the Alzheimer Foundation, which organises discussion groups for carers.

The work of the Centre's volunteers has unquestionably improved the quality of life of the elderly and their carers. Whether it has also meant that the elderly person can remain at home for longer, has not yet been demonstrated, but it may be assumed that it has.

There is a very low incidence of change among the volunteers and it also seems quite easy to recruit new ones. They themselves find the work, which is certainly not easy, a challenge. The contacts with others are also an encouragement.

Professional support is essential to an initiative such as the Call-in Centre. The volunteers like to see that everything is properly and carefully organised. It is an advantage here that there are two nursing homes which run the Centre. It lowers the threshold to the nursing home even if only because in the course of time the volunteer will come to know something about the nursing home. This helps people to make use of its services more readily.

The Centre also has good relations with other institutions: RIAGG, the social workers, general practitioners, district nurses and care workers. These good relations are very important; they increase the likelihood of smooth cooperation in the matter of work and referrals. The various institutions can also play a vital part in training the volunteers. Without such contacts the Centre's work would just hang in mid-air. The only trouble is that forming these networks takes a great deal of time and energy.

More information :

Oproepcentrale Nieuwe Waterweg-Noord

p/a Stichting Verpleeghuizen Niewe Waterweg-Noord

Voorberghlaan 35

NL-3123 AX Schiedam

11. Portugal

DAY CENTRES GO LOCAL
Under increasing pressure from carers

Under pressure from carers, the day centres for the elderly in Portugal have recently begun to offer their services more locally. This began with practical help on a small scale, but pressure from the carers is increasing. They feel that the day centres should offer more services, more different types and more flexible services. An excellent example of this development is the day centre in Santa Maria de Belém, a district of some thirteen thousand inhabitants in the capital, Lisbon.

During the 1970s, day centres came into existence in various parts of Portugal. The aim of these centres was to help elderly people to stay living in their own homes as long as possible and thus keep them out of institutions, or at least postpone their admission for a few years. The day centres target the elderly directly with their services. Indirectly this of course also benefits the carers. In recent times, this restricted aim has had to change somewhat due to the continuous ageing of the population. Additional services are being demanded from the day centres: help with the elderly at home and direct help to the families who care for old people at home.

Strangely enough, this last type of assistance is a new type of service in Portugal: the 'family' has of course played a major role through the centuries in looking after the old people but only now are the day centres and other institutions beginning to appreciate this.

Services offered

The day centre in Santa Maria de Belém is part of Misericordia de Lisboa, formerly a private charity but now a public social service institution in Lisbon. The day centre was once a club for the elderly. Under pressure from the elderly themselves and from the carers, the centre has rapidly begun to engage in other activities in recent years. The present services may be roughly described as 'supportive'. They help to enable carers – to the best of their abilities – to keep on doing their work without the help of more professional institutions.

The exact content of the services offered by the day centre depends on the situation of the elderly person. The day centre will assist by sending in professional social workers and home helps. But voluntary workers also play a part, even if only for odd jobs. In addition, the elderly can make use of the other services at the centre itself such as the restaurant and the laundry.

As soon as anyone makes a request to the centre, a social worker pays a visit to assess the situation at home. He or she will also make contact with other agencies in the health service but also, if necessary, with the local housing authority. It is also the social worker's responsibility to draw up a plan of whatever care the person needs.

The home helps are mainly for the more practical work; they help people to get up and go to bed and with washing, they do the cleaning and cooking etc. This help is provided for a maximum of six hours a day. If more help is needed, the family must make its own arrangements; if this is not possible then admission is unavoidable. The day centre sets no limit on the period for which the assistance is provided. In addition to this practical support, the centre organises regular joint meetings for the professionals and the carers. The intention here is to provide mutual emotional support and to exchange information and advice.

Voluntary workers
In addition to professional workers, the centre can also draw upon workers from voluntary organisations. The latter support the carers by keeping the elderly person company for a few hours a week. What is interesting is that there are two kinds of volunteers. One group might be called the 'young elderly', being people between the ages of 60 and 75 who themselves visit the day centre and are capable of doing voluntary work. The other group is mainly made up of young students who work for the centre in their free time. They support the carers, mainly by offering to sit-in for a few hours a day in their homes.

Target group
The services of the day centre are intended for the carers themselves - relatives, friends or neighbours - who look after the elderly in need of care. It is usually the carer who calls upon the day centre for help. Often this is a spouse who is also quite old and may be in poor health, so that he or she is no longer able to give the care required. It may, however, be a daughter(-in-law) or other family member who requests help. Then the problem is usually that the combination of their work outside the home, a normal family life and the care of the elderly person is becoming too heavy a burden. Neighbours and friends can help on a limited scale by keeping the elderly company, doing some of the shopping or accompanying them to visit the doctor. But if the elderly person suddenly becomes much more dependent, they are forced to ask for help from some other agency.

Internal organisation
As already mentioned, the day centre in Santa Maria de Belém is part of the Misericordia de Lisboa. This organisation has quite a lot of property which brings in an income; in addition it receives funding from the Portuguese state lottery and from the Toto. The day centre is mainly financed from these income sources. In addition the elderly who make use of it and their families make their own contribution. The services of both the professional and the voluntary workers are free.

On the other hand, the centre also assumes that carers, relatives, friends and neighbours, give their services for nothing. But neighbours who take over part of the work of the home help - for instance do the washing or cook a meal - may receive some small payment.

The day centre is managed by a social worker. The work is done by home helps who receive extra training at the centre for their work with the elderly. There are also a couple of domestic workers at the centre.

The centre has no need to advertise. This is partly because Misericordia de Lisboa is well known in the neighbourhood and the day centre takes advantage of this. In addition, the centre is of the open type; if anything is organised it is announced in places where people are likely to see it. The hospital in the neighbourhood - from which the centre receives good cooperation - also functions as a communi-cations channel.

More activities needed

As more and more carers called upon the centre for help, more staff had to be engaged and trained. In recruiting them the centre tried as far as possible to take advantage of the existence of young mothers in the neighbourhood. These are often foreign nationals. This sometimes - and more often than they would have liked - put the continuity of the care at risk. After all, these women themselves have young children and so they are not always available. The result was that recruitment do not go so well and there is still a staff shortage. Added to this, the young mothers from other countries were not always sufficiently integrated in the Portuguese community to be of much help to the elderly natives.

The carers themselves are quite enthusiastic about the new activities provided by the day centre. The help and information they receive, they say, gives them a feeling of security and emotional support. This means that they can cope better with their work and thus keep on doing it for longer.

It is interesting that carers seem to have this feeling only after they have been making use of the centre's services for some time. If the elderly person suddenly becomes much more dependent on them, their first reaction is still one of helplessness; in such a situation they still ask first for the patient to be admitted.

Experiences

What are the conclusions we may draw from this Portuguese experiment in carer support? First of all, that it is important and useful; it enables carers at least to look after very dependent elderly people for longer and under better conditions in their own homes. The fact that the carers themselves asked for it, says enough. This also has its disadvantages. For example, no research has ever been done into the actual needs on the ground. There is therefore no insight into the scope of these. In addition it also appears urgently necessary to provide carers with information or even to train them in the proper care of heavily dependent old people.

A separate problem is that the day centre is only open during office hours, every day from nine to six. Outside these hours the work of caring all falls back on the shoulders of the carers. In view of the problems which this may sometimes cause, there really ought to be a 24-hour, 7-day support service available. For this purpose there would have to be some institution in Santa Maria de Belém which could provide temporary residential care for the elderly. The carers could then get a break or take a holiday.

==
More information :

Santa Casa da Misericordia de Lisboa
Acçao Social
Largo Trinidade Coelho
P-1200 Lisboa
Tel: 351 1 3460361

Associação Portuguesa dos Familiares e Amigos dos Doentes Alzheimer
Rua Antonio Saldanha 11
P-1000 Lisboa
Tel: 351 1 7934480
==

12. United Kingdom

THE PINES

A home providing respite care in a small town

What do you do if you are a nurse and you cannot find a suitable place for your sick mother in one of the existing facilities? Then you set one up yourself. At least, that is how 'The Pines', a respite home for the elderly in Appleby-in-Westmorland came about. The same nurse and her husband are still running this home.

Target group and services provided

What does The Pines offer? First of all, long-term nursing care for twenty people. In addition, the home has one bed for temporary admissions and three day-care places. If necessary, the day care can be extended and there are plans to double the capacity for short- stay care, so that soon there will be two beds available. The residents at The Pines are elderly people who have been referred to a nursing home. This fact is not unimportant if the home is have official recognition and funding. The average age of the residents is 80+.

Although The Pines is basically a nursing home for long-term care, it also offers a range of other services: not merely respite care and day care but also care in the patient's own home and support (including emotional support) for carers.

The intention is to make the care provided as flexible as possible. This is why the people at The Pines always have an extended interview with the carer and the elderly person first, to find out what exactly is required. For example, the user may ask for help during the night hours. But also if the carer needs a short break, that can also be arranged. The length of the stay will also be discussed at these interviews.

Internal organisation

The reason why they set up The Pines in the first place has not been forgotten by the couple who run it. They have continued to offer care on a very flexible basis because they know this is what the local community needs.

The home itself has a fairly normal type of hierarchy. The owners themselves are the managers. They have delegated some responsibilities to staff members who work directly with the clients. A number of employees, the 'care workers', see to the social side of the service while a qualified nurse looks after the medical side.

A residential place costs £ 260 a week, day care costs £ 12 per day. The cost of the other services depends on the package agreed. The whole package must not exceed £ 260 a week, however. The Pines makes a small profit on the long-stay patients; this means that other services can be offered on a non-profit basis.

The residents enjoy a large measure of independence. They have a good deal of personal choice, are involved in the decision-making and do as much for themselves as they are still capable of doing. There has been a conscious attempt to avoid institutionalisation.

A local service
This a very local service which is regarded as part of the community. All the staff, including the owners/managers, are local people. This has the effect of breaking down some of the barriers which can exist between formal and informal carers.

The Pines is very accessible; there is no formal bureaucracy to negotiate. Elderly people and their carers can make a direct request for service. Their needs are discussed and appropriate care negotiated. An important feature is that carers are integral to this process, with their needs also being addressed. If they wish, they can at any time contribute their share of help. This may help them to feel less guilty, for example, for not just having dumped 'their' elderly person somewhere.

The Pines has no need to advertise. Everyone in the community knows what they offer. Not only the families themselves, but also the Church and GPs function as channels of communication.

The Pines has good links with health and social care agencies locally. This includes the district office of the Social Services Department, Crossroads and a local residential centre for the elderly. Links with other groups include the church, the Rotary Club and local schools. These may be a source of referrals or of practical and social support.

In addition, the home is registered with the District Health Authority. This is a legal requirement of all private nursing homes. Under the terms of the registration it is subject to an annual inspection.

Experiences
Problems which sometimes seem to attach themselves to being cared for do not exist at The Pines. The elderly person does not have the stigma of being a nursing home patient; he or she remains as independent as in his/her own home. Through the informal and flexible nature of the home and because the elderly and their carers are always involved in the plans, decisions and, if they wish, in lending a hand as well, the links with the community are preserved. Short-term, respite care can be planned in such as way as to disrupt everyday routines as little as possible. This also helps the carers to feel less 'guilty'.

One problem which has emerged is in relation to The Pines' philosophy of 'risk taking' and the degree to which this is actually allowed to develop. It challenges the 'common sense' view that residential care removes risk. At The Pines, for example, an elderly man has been allowed to visit the local pub at lunchtime, something which would be regarded as having an unacceptably high degree of risk by most comparable services in the UK. In cases where the carer is concerned that the elderly person should not be exposed to risks, some negotiation may be necessary. However, the staff of The Pines take the view that, without risk-taking, residential care may become dominated by surveillance.

Meaning for carers
Carers are able to obtain freedom within their caring role by use of the respite service. They can obtain a break, and be involved in choosing when and for how long it will be. Respite residential care can be difficult for the elderly person at first but many of them seem happy to make return visits. Moreover, because the facility is homely and part of the local community, there is not the same sense of 'putting someone away' which so

often is felt by carers. It enables carers to feel that their caring is shared without losing control or having their own role undermined.

Many carers regard a permanent stay as the only realistic course in the long term. The Pines offers an alternative which, because of its ties with the local community and its unique approach, is most attractive. In this sense it is a good example of the development of small- scale private care facilities. The care offered by The Pines is never a fixed package but can be adjusted to meet the needs of the elderly person and his/her carer. The various services are interchangeable. Short-term care may involve an overnight stay or simply day care, or even care in the person's home. The difference between short-term and long-term care in the home is dictated by the needs of the user and not by the structure of the facility. In this respect the respite services are not really separate from continuing care but have evolved from it.

In part, the positive aspects of The Pines come from the personal motivation and commitment of the owners/managers and in part from the local base in the community of a small rural town. The size, personal involvement and local basis all combine to make the non- institutional pattern of care possible. These factors also mean that innovation and flexibility, including the close involvement of elderly people and carers, are entirely the responsibility of the individuals who are involved. Their accountability is not to a service agency but to the direct service users and more indirectly to the community of which they are a part.

Transferability
Can such a typically British initiative be used as a model for others wishing to set up a similar home elsewhere in the United Kingdom or in Europe? This is dependent on two factors, firstly the funding and the extent of state involvement, and secondly, whether the particular approach opted for by the owners can be implemented elsewhere.

Although the owners provided the initial capital from their own resources, the rates paid by the users cover the running costs. Some users receive an allowance to assist with their expenses. In this sense there is a certain element of state support. Without this support the potential clientele of

The Pines would be a smaller one. As a matter of fact, The Pines can offer its other services on a non-profit basis partly because the British Social Service scales of fees for nursing homes are higher for residential care without nursing input in 'rest homes'. State recognition is required for registration as a nursing home.

The personal commitments of the owners/managers and other staff are combined with current developments in professional thinking about group care for older people. The location in a close-knit rural community makes possible a greater degree of flexibility than might be anticipated in a larger urban area. This also makes respite care more acceptable to the elderly people.

With these provisos in mind, The Pines serves as a good illustration of the development of formal care services which make connections with carers' needs, and it embodies the principles of tailoring the service to the service users and maintaining as much of what is valued in ordinary life as possible. These aspects are transferable to a wide variety of contexts, elsewhere in the UK and in other EC countries.

===
More information :
Ms. M. Baker
"The Pines"
Bongate
Appleby-in-Westmorland
UK-Cumbria CA16 6HN
===

13. United Kingdom

THE CARERS' NATIONAL ASSOCIATION
A national organisation for carers

For over twenty-five years there has been an organisation in the United Kingdom for carers. At first this was a National Council, a forceful pressure group representing the interests of single women who were also caring for someone, usually a relative. In 1988 this organisation joined up the the 'Association of Carers' which had been formed some years previously, to form the Carers' National Association and become one of the strongest associations for carers in Europe. The Carers' National Association now employs dozens of people and its annual budget is over £450,000.

The Carers' National Association has four objectives:

1. **To keep carers informed**
    the Association publishes pamphlets and booklets on such subjects as social security, facilities and available services. Anyone can order these publications; the members of the Association also receive a regular newsletter.
2. **To support carers**
    This support is mainly in the form of a network of local and regional groups. Here, carers can exchange ideas and discuss problems in an atmosphere of mutual understanding. Local groups can call upon the Association head office for help but mainly run the groups themselves, usually without paid staff.
3. **To lobby for change**
    In order to improve the position of carers, the Association lobbies at national level, through the media and in parliament. There is a need also to affect professionals' thinking, through an impact on training. The aim in both cases is get carers seen as experts, resources, people with their own special needs and partners in care all at the same time.
4. **To encourage carers**
    Carers should recognise their own needs. The Carers' Association encourages such recognition partly through the media and partly by

other means. Nationally and locally, there are campaigns and information days; locally, also, members work with professionals to make them more aware of and responsive to carers' needs.

The members
Membership of the Carers' National Association costs £Stg 3.00 a year. It is not considered reasonable to ask for more from a group of whom most suffer financial hardship.

The members are drawn from all shades of political opinion but the Association avoids strong links with any particular party. Some members are critical of this neutral stance while others feel the Association is too political. It does its best to keep a balance.

Over eighty per cent of the members are women and over a quarter are aged over seventy. This does not mean there are no young members. In 1989 a project was launched for 'Young Carers', who often remain unknown because there is no provision at all for them. Their parents are often against their seeking help from outside, too, in case they become labelled as a problem family. The Carers' Association carried out research in the Merseyside region, after which development work began in various other parts of the country. The young people were very glad of this and one of them, in the 1990/91 Annual Report of the Association, is quoted as saying: "Seeing my own experiences as the subject of discussion has given me great strength. I now realise that it is unacceptable to place children and young people in difficult situations for which many adults would have no solutions."

Internal organisation
The Association is run by a national committee, elected from the membership, with paid staff centrally and regionally. What is just as important is the network of national, regional and local branches of the Carers' Association. There are 85 branches throughout the UK, some as small as 12 members and some with a membership of over a hundred. The branches aim principally to provide mutual support and assistance ('the feeling that there is someone nearby who understands') and to promote the needs of carers in the local area.

In 1991 the Association began an extensive 'Branching Out' campaign with the aim of creating more local groups. One result of this was the impact in Scotland, for instance - a country of five million inhabitants, three-quarters of a million of whom are carers but which had only four organisations. In the Strathclyde region, a large area which is home to half the population of Scotland, the Association was able to set up a strong development team with the help of twelve people, and a forum for carers, while in many other areas groups were set up. There are 'start-up' grants available to new branches and some staff support in development.

The Carers' Association is mainly accessible through the local branches but the national centre will provide information or advice in writing (within two weeks) or by telephone.

Cooperation is seen as vital to provide an effective collective voice for the carers. The Association uses the existing channels of information, such as GPs, as much as possible. It also works closely with the Alzheimer society and with Crossroads, an organisation specially set up to support carers, for example, by taking over their duties for a spell. Along with seventeen other groups, the Association takes an active part in the platform organisation Carers' Alliance.

Effect
Is the Carers' National Association capable of achieving the four objectives it has set itself? According to itself, it does, for the most part.

There is plenty of information available, both general and national and also more specific and local. Both in printed form and via the telephone advisory service. Television is also a useful channel for communications; the Association collaborates almost every year in making programmes about caring. It is important to try to keep the information as accessible as possible, neither relying on jargon nor being patronising.

The Association is also anxious to provide information on the support it offers to carers. The problem is, however, that this support is not available everywhere. Rural areas, for example, are difficult to serve. The

'Branching Out' project was mainly set up to fill this gap. In some parts of the country welfare workers and district nurses are involved in setting up self-help groups. The Carers' National Association would like to cooperate more often with these groups.

The effect of lobbying - its third objective - is more clearly visible. The Association has succeeded in getting carers placed higher on the agenda with policy-makers and politicians. In research on the subject of municipal health care, the Association was expressly asked for its opinion. And also in the subsequent policy statement and in the new National Health Service Act, the needs of carers are explicitly addressed. This does not mean, however, that the Association has it all its own way in relation to the UK health care system. The Association was disappointed in 1991 when the government took so little account of the carers in drafting new legislation concerning benefits and work for the disabled. One example: a person caring for two people and spending 35 hours a week on this work, receives no Invalid Care Allowance. Yet a person caring for over 35 hours a week for one person does.

The Association was also dismayed that the updating of the municipal health care system was partly postponed. Until it is completely implemented the Association will be concentrating on the content of the new municipal schemes.

Many local authorities in fact consult the organisations of carers on the subject of their draft plans. Together with the authorities, the Association is seeking for the best way to bring carers' views to light. The Ministry of Health grant-aided a project in North-West England which resulted in a practical handbook for consulting with carers. In drawing up the compulsory regulations regarding complaints, now in force, the Association also collaborated with the Ministry of Health.

In realising their fourth objective - to encourage carers to recognise their own needs - the Association is making efforts in three areas which have already been dealt with above: information, support and lobbying. Through such efforts the notion of caring has already become more familiar. Good relations with the professional care services have been found important here; after all carers rarely meet each other but have much more contact with general practitioners, social workers and district nurses.

Experiences
If there are any differences of opinion within the Association, these are often over the question of whether the Association ought to be more political, or just the opposite.

The Carers' National Association represents the interests of carers. These are not always an extension of those of the patient. In this respect, it is important to emphasise the idea of partnership, consultation and cooperation. This requires everyone who is engaged in providing help or care to alter his/her attitudes and methods a little.

The unpaid voluntary workers - themselves carers - are the ones who keep the local branches going. These local branches can certainly be set up elsewhere in Europe. The problem is that carers will only start to set up a local group if they actually see themselves as carers. For this, information seems to be needed, together with various other activities from a national association.

Finally, the Carers' National Association has developed out of the British tradition of voluntary caring work. The main features of this are 'shared care' and 'mutual advantage' through information and emotional and psychological support. Those wishing to set up an association for carers elsewhere in Europe will do well to take into account the context in relation to voluntary action in their own country.

===
More information :
Ms. Jill Pitkeathley
Carer's National Association
20/25 Glasshouse Yard
London EC1A 4JS
United Kingdom
===

14. Ireland

CHARTER OF THE RIGHTS OF CARERS

The cases in this book show that there are projects to support carers all over Europe. Most of the time, without being paid, carers do an enormous amount of work by caring for other people (usually elderly people). In view of these efforts, the attention for practical, social and economic support is rather meagre.
The examples from Belgium and the United Kingdom show that carers start to get organized. They take up the cudgel for all individual carers who are too busy caring to look after their interests. They plead that more political attention should be paid to the support and relief of carers. They keep emphasizing the social importance of care. In all EC member states national governments will have to form policies to support and relief carers. A political strengthening of the position of the carer is also wanted at a European level.

A good example of a project to support carers and to strengthen their political position comes from Ireland. This example can be followed in all EC member states and can also be supported at a European level.
For some time now, in Ireland a women's volunteer organization (Soroptomist International) and researchers of the National College of Industrial Relations have been engaged in laying down the rights of the carer in a charter. Of course this should be more than a pious declaration of intent. Therefore it is gratifying that the initiators have succeeded in winning over the Irish government to their cause. They started to work on this charter by making an observation that can also be made elsewhere in Europe: the family is, and will always be, the most reliable source of care for the elderly, the disabled and for people who have chronical illnesses. Most people who need care live at home and are not in hospitals, nursing homes or other institutions. Families are constantly showing a tremendous capacity to adapt themselves to the needs of sick family members, in all kinds of situations. In Ireland itself about 100.000 carers are involved, all over Europe there must be millions of them. They work long hours and generally carry the financial burden themselves. Many of them are old themselves and sometimes even sick.

This army of carers makes efforts which can hardly be calculated, neither socially nor economically. If they would not be there governments would have to spend much more money on health care and home help. The conclusion is inevitable: in view of these enormous efforts some rights for the carers would be justified. A 'Charter of the rights of carers' is needed.

Step by step
This idea began to take root at an Irish conference about care at the end of the eighties. The Irish department of the women's volunteer organization Soroptomist International and the National College of Industrial Relations took up the gauntlet and the charter was drawn up step by step: the volunteers by setting up a nationwide support programme, the researchers by systematically describing the experiences that were gained.
On 20 April 1991 the Charter could be offered to the Irish health secretary, Chris Flood. Afterwards he made sure that the charter was not tucked away in a drawer. For instance, he sent a copy to the chairmen of all Irish health regions, with the request to take it into account when reorganizing the health care.
Neither have the authors of the Charter been sitting around and doing nothing afterwards. The support programmes for carers in Ireland have been expanded, the press has continuously been harassed and the Charter was introduced in the European parliament.

Guidelines
What exactly does this Charter say? Sixteen provisions are formulated. Separately and in itself they are not startling, but together they provide the guidelines to which a policy that aims at a better position of the carer has to comply with.

Carers' Charter
1. Carers have the right to be recognised for the central role which they play in community care and in creating a community of caring.
2. Carers have the right to acknowledge and address their own needs for personal fulfilment.
3. Carers have the right to acknowledge and address their own needs in relation to their contribution to their family and community.
4. Carers have the right to practical help in carrying out the tasks of

caregiving, including domestic help, home adaptations, appliances, incontinence services and help with transport.
5. Carers have the right to support services, e.g. public health nurses, day centres and home helps in providing medical, personal and domestic care.
6. Carers have the right to respite care both for short spells as in day hospitals and for longer periods to enable them to have time for themselves.
7. Carers have the right to emotional and moral support.
8. Carers have the right to financial support and recompense which does not preclude carers taking employment or in sharing care with other people.
9. Carers have the right to regular assessment and review of their needs and those of the people for whom they care.
10. Carers have the right to easy access to information and advice.
11. Carers have the right to expect involvement of all family members.
12. Carers have the right to have counselling made available to them at different stages of the caring process including bereavement counselling.
13. Carers have the right to skills' training and development of their potential.
14. Carers have the right to expect their families, public authorities and community members to provide a plan for services and support of carers, taking into account the unique demographic developments up to and beyond the year 2000.
15. Carers have the right to involvement at all levels of policy planning, to participate and contribute to the planning to the planning of an integrated and co-ordinated service of carers.
16. Carers have the right to have an infrastructure of care, a supportive network to which they can relate when the need arises.

Of course these rights do not solve all practical problems of a carer. A number of problems that can be found in highly developed countries are not mentioned in this Charter. In the Federal Republic for instance, the question whether and how emotional and practical help can be combined will remain a problem. And in Holland and elsewhere it will remain a difficult problem to teach professionals not to fall back on patronizing in their

contact with carers. In a later stage the less developed welfare states might get similar problems and in that case the Charter must be expanded.
Something that is not mentioned either is the relation between state governments and private institutions and the relationships between professionals. This enhances the clarity of the Charter. And perhaps it is good to tackle such problems per member state. Moreover: it is not the problem of carers how their rights are guaranteed. As long as they are guaranteed!
Something that is discussed tersely in the Charter is the social dimension of the individual burden of carers. Carers will probably always see their efforts and the relationship with a family member who needs care as a personal burden. On the one hand this is a good thing: otherwise they would never be able to make such great efforts. On the other hand this personalizing is the basis of the social invisibility (or: exploitation) of this group of people. Therefore it is a good thing that this personal relationship is discussed from another point of view.

Just like the example from Ireland the political recognition of the Rights of the Carer needs the support of politicians. It is a challenge to the European Community to formulate the Rights of the Carer as a touchstone for its policy.

===
More information :
Ms. Joyce O'Connor
National College of Industrial Relations
Sandford Road
Ranelagh
Dublin 6
Tel: 353 1 972917
===

European Foundation for the Improvement of Living and Working Conditions

Family Care of the Older Elderly: Casebook of Initiatives

Luxembourg: Office for Official Publications of the European Communities

1993 – 88 p. – 16 x 23.4 cm

ISBN 92-826-6572-0

Price (excluding VAT) in Luxembourg: ECU 10

Venta y suscripciones • Salg og abonnement • Verkauf und Abonnement • Πωλήσεις και συνδρομές
Sales and subscriptions • Vente et abonnements • Vendita e abbonamenti
Verkoop en abonnementen • Venda e assinaturas

BELGIQUE / BELGIË

**Moniteur belge /
Belgisch Staatsblad**
Rue de Louvain 42 / Leuvenseweg 42
B-1000 Bruxelles / B-1000 Brussel
Tél. (02) 512 00 26
Fax (02) 511 01 84

Autres distributeurs /
Overige verkooppunten

**Librairie européenne /
Europese boekhandel**
Rue de la Loi 244 / Wetstraat 244
B-1040 Bruxelles / B-1040 Brussel
Tél. (02) 231 04 35
Fax (02) 735 08 60

Jean de Lannoy
Avenue du Roi 202 / Koningslaan 202
B-1060 Bruxelles / B-1060 Brussel
Tél. (02) 538 51 69
Télex 63220 UNBOOK B
Fax (02) 538 08 41

Document delivery:

Credoc
Rue de la Montagne 34 / Bergstraat 34
Bte 11 / Bus 11
B-1000 Bruxelles / B-1000 Brussel
Tél. (02) 511 69 41
Fax (02) 513 31 95

DANMARK

J. H. Schultz Information A/S
Herstedvang 10-12
DK-2620 Albertslund
Tlf. 43 63 23 00
Fax (Sales) 43 63 19 69
Fax (Management) 43 63 19 49

DEUTSCHLAND

Bundesanzeiger Verlag
Breite Straße 78-80
Postfach 10 05 34
D-50445 Köln
Tel. (02 21) 20 29-0
Telex ANZEIGER BONN 8 882 595
Fax 2 02 92 78

GREECE/ΕΛΛΑΔΑ

G.C. Eleftheroudakis SA
International Bookstore
Nikis Street 4
GR-10563 Athens
Tel. (01) 322 63 23
Telex 219410 ELEF
Fax 323 98 21

ESPAÑA

Boletín Oficial del Estado
Trafalgar, 29
E-28071 Madrid
Tel. (91) 538 22 95
Fax (91) 538 23 49

Mundi-Prensa Libros, SA
Castelló, 37
E-28001 Madrid
Tel. (91) 431 33 99 (Libros)
　　　431 32 22 (Suscripciones)
　　　435 36 37 (Dirección)
Télex 49370-MPLI-E
Fax (91) 575 39 98

Sucursal:

Librería Internacional AEDOS
Consejo de Ciento, 391
E-08009 Barcelona
Tel. (93) 488 34 92
Fax (93) 487 76 59

**Llibreria de la Generalitat
de Catalunya**
Rambla dels Estudis, 118 (Palau Moja)
E-08002 Barcelona
Tel. (93) 302 68 35
　　　302 64 62
Fax (93) 302 12 99

FRANCE

**Journal officiel
Service des publications
des Communautés européennes**
26, rue Desaix
F-75727 Paris Cedex 15
Tél. (1) 40 58 75 00
Fax (1) 40 58 77 00

IRELAND

Government Supplies Agency
4-5 Harcourt Road
Dublin 2
Tel. (1) 66 13 111
Fax (1) 47 80 645

ITALIA

Licosa SpA
Via Duca di Calabria, 1/1
Casella postale 552
I-50125 Firenze
Tel. (055) 64 54 15
Fax 64 12 57
Telex 570466 LICOSA I

GRAND-DUCHÉ DE LUXEMBOURG

Messageries du livre
5, rue Raiffeisen
L-2411 Luxembourg
Tél. 40 10 20
Fax 40 10 24 01

NEDERLAND

SDU Overheidsinformatie
Externe Fondsen
Postbus 20014
2500 EA's-Gravenhage
Tel. (070) 37 89 911
Fax (070) 34 75 778

PORTUGAL

Imprensa Nacional
Casa da Moeda, EP
Rua D. Francisco Manuel de Melo, 5
P-1092 Lisboa Codex
Tel. (01) 69 34 14

**Distribuidora de Livros
Bertrand, Ld.ª**
Grupo Bertrand, SA
Rua das Terras dos Vales, 4-A
Apartado 37
P-2700 Amadora Codex
Tel. (01) 49 59 050
Telex 15798 BERDIS
Fax 49 60 255

UNITED KINGDOM

HMSO Books (Agency section)
HMSO Publications Centre
51 Nine Elms Lane
London SW8 5DR
Tel. (071) 873 9090
Fax 873 8463
Telex 29 71 138

ÖSTERREICH

**Manz'sche Verlags-
und Universitätsbuchhandlung**
Kohlmarkt 16
A-1014 Wien
Tel. (0222) 531 61-133
Telex 112 500 BOX A
Fax (0222) 531 61-181

SUOMI/FINLAND

Akateeminen Kirjakauppa
Keskuskatu 1
PO Box 128
SF-00101 Helsinki
Tel. (0) 121 41
Fax (0) 121 44 41

NORGE

Narvesen Info Center
Bertrand Narvesens vei 2
PO Box 6125 Etterstad
N-0602 Oslo 6
Tel. (22) 57 33 00
Telex 79668 NIC N
Fax (22) 68 19 01

SVERIGE

BTJ AB
Traktorvägen 13
S-22100 Lund
Tel. (046) 18 00 00
Fax (046) 18 01 25
　　　　30 79 47

SCHWEIZ / SUISSE / SVIZZERA

OSEC
Stampfenbachstraße 85
CH-8035 Zürich
Tel. (01) 365 54 49
Fax (01) 365 54 11

ČESKÁ REPUBLIKA

NIS ČR
Havelkova 22
130 00 Praha 3
Tel. (2) 235 84 46
Fax (2) 235 97 88

MAGYARORSZÁG

Euro-Info-Service
Club Sziget
Margitsziget
1138 Budapest
Tel./Fax 1 111 60 61
　　　　 1 111 62 16

POLSKA

Business Foundation
ul. Krucza 38/42
00-512 Warszawa
Tel. (22) 21 99 93, 628-28 82
International Fax & Phone
(0-39) 12-00-77

ROMÂNIA

Euromedia
65, Strada Dionisie Lupu
70184 Bucuresti
Tel./Fax 0 12 96 46

BÃLGARIJA

Europress Klassica BK Ltd
66, bd Vitosha
1463 Sofia
Tel./Fax 2 52 74 75

RUSSIA

CCEC
9,60-letiya Oktyabrya Avenue
117312 Moscow
Tel./Fax (095) 135 52 27

CYPRUS

**Cyprus Chamber of Commerce and
Industry**
Chamber Building
38 Grivas Dhigenis Ave
3 Deligiorgis Street
PO Box 1455
Nicosia
Tel. (2) 449500/462312
Fax (2) 458630

MALTA

Miller distributors Ltd
Scots House, M.A. Vassalli street
PO Box 272
Valletta
Tel. 24 73 01
Fax 23 49 14

TÜRKIYE

**Pres Gazete Kitap Dergi
Pazarlama Dağitim Ticaret ve sanayi
AŞ**
Narlibahçe Sokak N. 15
Istanbul-Cağaloğlu
Tel. (1) 520 92 96 - 528 55 66
Fax 520 64 57
Telex 23822 DSVO-TR

ISRAEL

ROY International
PO Box 13056
41 Mishmar Hayarden Street
Tel. Aviv 61130
Tel. 3 496 108
Fax 3 544 60 39

UNITED STATES OF AMERICA/
CANADA

UNIPUB
4611-F Assembly Drive
Lanham, MD 20706-4391
Tel. Toll Free (800) 274 4888
Fax (301) 459 0056

CANADA

Subscriptions only
Uniquement abonnements

Renouf Publishing Co. Ltd
1294 Algoma Road
Ottawa, Ontario K1B 3W8
Tel. (613) 741 43 33
Fax (613) 741 54 39
Telex 0534783

AUSTRALIA

Hunter Publications
58A Gipps Street
Collingwood
Victoria 3066
Tel. (3) 417 5361
Fax (3) 419 7154

JAPAN

Kinokuniya Company Ltd
17-7 Shinjuku 3- Chome
Shinjuku-ku
Tokyo 160-91
Tel. (03) 3439-0121

Journal Department
PO Box 55 Chitose
Tokyo 156
Tel. (03) 3439-0124

SOUTH-EAST ASIA

Legal Library Services Ltd
STK Agency
Robinson Road
PO Box 1817
Singapore 9036

SOUTH AFRICA

Safto
5th Floor, Export House
Cnr Maude & West Streets
Sandton 2146
Tel. (011) 883-3737
Fax (011) 883-6569

AUTRE PAYS
OTHER COUNTRIES
ANDERE LÄNDER

**Office des publications officielles
des Communautés européennes**
2, rue Mercier
L-2985 Luxembourg
Tél. 499 28 -1
Télex PUBOF LU 1324 b
Fax 48 85 73/48 68 17